last in the **evening**

OSHO

last in the **evening**

365 Relaxing Moments
to Enter the Night Consciously

Originally published as *A Must for Contemplation before Sleep*, revised edition.

The quotations in this book are taken from transcripts of meetings with
Osho where he gave guidance to individuals about meditation, life and work.
The complete OSHO text archive can be found via the online OSHO Library
at www.osho.com/library

OSHO is a registered trademark of OSHO International Foundation
www.osho.com/trademarks

OSHO MEDIA INTERNATIONAL
New York • Zurich • Mumbai
an imprint of
OSHO INTERNATIONAL
www.osho.com/oshointernational

Distributed by Publishers Group Worldwide
www.pgw.com

Library of Congress Catalog-In-Publication Data is available

Printed in India by Manipal Technologies Limited, Karnataka

ISBN: 978-1-938755-83-5
This title is also available in eBook format ISBN: 978-0-88050-620-5

contents

introduction

The words on the following pages are extracted from intimate meetings, where the contemporary mystic, Osho, talks with people from all walks of life. It was at Osho's suggestion that this, and its companion volume, *First in the Morning*, were compiled. The books have been planned in such a way that each day has a particular theme, and the subject of the morning and evening complement each other. So, *Last in the Evening* can be read alone, or in combination with the morning book.

The passages in this volume have been specially chosen for the nighttime – reading one before sleep can provide the perfect way to end the day. The book contains 365 passages which have been designed to be read chronologically, rather than randomly.

In this book, Osho sometimes refers to "sannyas" or "sannyasins." As Osho uses this term, sannyas simply means making a decision to bring self-awareness into your life, a commitment to give time to the exploration and celebration of the inner: *"We know much that is rubbish: we know everything about the moon and the sun and the earth and we know history and geography, but we know nothing about ourselves. We know nothing about the knower – and that should be the primary concern of any real education. Sannyas is the beginning of a real education. Fundamentally you have to become aware of yourself, of who you are. And only you can do that."*

Reading the passages in this book is in itself a form of

contemplation because, as Osho says, the words of a mystic are not part of any theory to be accepted or refuted; the reader is not asked to be a follower or a believer. In fact, it is not even the words themselves that are of significance, but rather what the words convey.

"[The mystic's] words carry a silence around them, his words are not noisy. His words have a melody, a rhythm, a music, and at the very core of his words is utter silence. If you can penetrate his words you will come across infinite silence.

"But to penetrate the words of a buddha, the way is not analysis, the way is not argument, the way is not discussing. The way is falling in rapport with him, becoming attuned with him, being in syn-chronicity with him… In that attunement, in that at-onement, one enters the very core of the master's words. And there you will not find any sound, any noise; there you will find absolute silence. And to taste it is to understand the master.

"The meaning of the word is not important, remember, but the silence of the word."

Osho,
The Dhammapada: The Way of the Buddha, Volume 3

DAY 1

The world is suffering so much because for the first time in the history of human consciousness, man has lost track of godliness. Nobody has ever suffered like us. People have been poor in the past, very poor; people have starved, but people have never been so poor spiritually. People have never starved spiritually as much as today. My whole work is to give you back an insight into godliness. Unless man becomes rooted in godliness again, he has no future.

DAY 2

Man has the potential of becoming a song of love, a dance of love, but very few people, very rare people, transform their potential into the actual. People are born as seeds and almost all die as seeds; their lives remain nothing but a long experiment in futility. And the older they grow the more frustrated they become, naturally, because all their hopes are being shattered, all their desires are bringing nothing but tears, agony, anguish. As time passes, they become aware that whatever they have been doing with their lives has been of no value. How can they sing? How can they dance? How can they feel grateful to existence? It is impossible.

My observation is that people go to temples and synagogues and churches only out of fear, not out of love. And older people go more often because they have become more afraid of death. They don't go to church or to a temple because they have known something tremendously valuable in life, but because life is slipping out of their hands. The great darkness of death is coming closer and they are afraid. They want someone to protect them.

Now they know that their money is not going to be with them, their friends are not going to be with them, their families will leave them. Out of desperation they start clinging to the idea of a God. But this is not out of love and it is not out of gratitude. And a God born out of fear is a false God. A God born out of love is a true God.

My whole effort here is to make windows into God available so that you don't go to God out of fear, so that you can go through the experience of beauty, through the experience of creativity, through the experience of love. And when a person goes through these experiences, the contact is tremendous, transforming. A single living contact with godliness is enough – you will never be the same again.

DAY 3

When you start going in, mind is left behind. It can't go inside with you, it can only go with you outside. It has only one possibility, it is one-dimensional. Mind makes a person a warrior, in the political sense. Meditation makes him a warrior in the religious sense.

So become an inner warrior – much has to be conquered there. There is much darkness that has to be dispelled, much unconsciousness that has to be transformed, much raw energy that has to be purified.

It is a great task, the greatest that life gives you to fulfill. The great challenge is to become a fully grown-up person, to come to the crescendo of your potentiality, to reach the highest peak, the Everest of your consciousness. Then, for the first time, one really starts living.

DAY 4

Love has to be just your quality. Become loving, and one day it happens that you are simply love; not even loving but love. That is the day of great revelation. In that very moment the dewdrop disappears into the ocean and becomes the ocean.

In religious terminology, in religious jargon, it has been

called God-realization. If one likes religious jargon one can use that word, otherwise it is far more beautiful to say that one becomes oceanic; it is far more poetic. Priests have contaminated the word *God* too much, quarreling around the word *God* for so many centuries that the very word immediately raises a thousand and one questions. It simply creates more and more arguments and controversies. But the word in itself was beautiful when used for the first time; it simply represented the beyond, the vast beyond.

Now it does not represent the beyond anymore. Even the beyond has been exploited by priests. Priests are the most cunning people. They have made God a Christian God, a Hindu God, a Mohammedan God. Nothing more absurd can be done, it is the ultimate in absurdity. God cannot be Hindu or Jewish or Buddhist. God simply means vastness, and to make vastness Christian is to make it small. Any adjective will limit it. God has to be without an adjective. It simply means the infinite existence, the unbounded. And love will give you the first taste of it.

DAY 5

The moment you say "God," it seems a very faraway thing. That's what they have been saying down the centuries: God is somewhere above – in the sky very, very far away. But when you say "love," it is very close to the heart. All those priests are cunning and crafty. They have been trying to prove that God is far away because only if he is far away can they be the representatives of God, the mediators, the agents. If God is far away, that makes the pope relevant; if God is very close to your heart, what is the need of a pope? There is no need of anybody to mediate between you and God. If God is the heartbeat, then the Vatican becomes irrelevant, then all the churches and all the priests lose their profession. They have a beautiful profession, the most prestigious, powerful; who wants to lose prestige and power? The moment you use the word *God*, it gives you a sense of person. God becomes limited, becomes defined.

But love is not a person; it is a quality, a presence. It is a fragrance, not a flower – more unlimited, more unbounded, more infinite.

When you say "God," you simply feel impotent: "What to do?" But if love is there, you can do something about it. It is your innermost nature to be loving; hence my whole teaching revolves around the word *love*.

Jesus says, "God is love." I say love is God.

DAY 6

Start doing things, small things, totally. You have gone for a walk: then be total in your walk. Enjoy it, as if life consists only of walking and nothing else, as if walking is the ultimate. You have gone to swim: then swim and forget everything. Then there is no past and no future, only you and the water and the present moment. In this way you will slowly, slowly learn the art of being total. Go on applying the same art to your whole life. One day the miracle happens, when all the parts melt into one unity. That unity is your soul, that harmony is your soul. And when you are in harmony you know that the whole of existence is in harmony. You know only that which you are. You can't know more than that.

To be in harmony within oneself is to know the ultimate harmony of existence. One can call it God, nirvana, truth, or one can be simply silent about it because no word is adequate. Nothing can express it, nothing can explain it. The mystery remains a mystery.

DAY 7

Let your love be unaddressed. Love the whole of existence; it is one reality. The trees and the mountains and the people are not really different. We all participate together, we exist in a deep harmony. We go on breathing in oxygen and breathing out carbon dioxide.

Trees go on breathing in carbon dioxide and breathing out oxygen. Now, without trees we will not be able to exist. We are joined together, we interpenetrate. And that's how the whole of existence is interlinked. So let your love be unaddressed – the trees, the stars, the mountains, the people, the animals. The point is not to whom you are loving, the point is that you are loving.

DAY 8

Man's well-being is with God. If we become rooted in God, we are whole and healthy. If we remain without God, we remain without roots, without nourishment. God is more a mother than a father, more a she than a he. It is just the male chauvinist attitude that has made him a he.

God is the earth, our nourishment, our well-being. And the whole of life is nothing but an exploration – an exploration of the source of our well-being.

DAY 9

One who is surrendered to existence need not say anything; the very surrender will transform his life. All that is needed on the part of the seeker is to drop the ego because the ego is the only cause of all our misery and sadness.

The ego is the only wall between us and existence. And it is not made of very substantial bricks either; it is just an idea, just hot air. Just a pinprick and the balloon can burst. It does not need much work; it only needs intelligence, a little understanding.

DAY 10

Man has to go beyond his will so that he can become part of the divine will. One has to drop one's own will; it is the whole trouble.

Once our will is dissolved, then godliness starts functioning through us. Then there is no misery, no anxiety. One is utterly relaxed; there is no difficulty.

All problems arise out of your will because will means fighting with the whole. It is struggle, and struggle is bound to bring tension. And you are doomed to fail; hence, however hard one fights, one knows deep down in the heart, deep down somewhere that it is futile. One cannot succeed against the whole.

One can succeed only *with* the whole, not against the whole. Sannyas means surrendering your will, going beyond it. And the moment you surrender your will, all is yours. Suddenly the whole universe opens its doors for you. All the mysteries become available to you, all the secrets are handed over to you, all the keys.

The paradox is, in surrendering the will you become the master. And in keeping the will and fighting for it, you will remain a slave.

DAY 11

People are hard. Life prepares them to be hard because life prepares them to fight. Slowly, slowly they lose all inner softness: they become rocklike. And a rocklike person is a dead person. He lives only in name, he does not truly live. True life consists of softness, vulnerability, openness. Don't be afraid of existence: existence cares for you, loves you. There is no need to fight with it.

Existence is ready to give more than you can ever ask for or you can ever imagine. But existence can give only if you are soft, vulnerable. If you are porous, it can enter from everywhere.

Be porous, be available to existence, unafraid. There is no need to be afraid. It is our existence, we belong to it; it belongs to us.

DAY 12

Buddha has tremendous beauty around him, an inexplicable grace, something very much of the beyond. And it became possible only because he never believed in the stupid idea of God. He went directly into the search, into the inquiry of the existence of bliss. And because he became blissful he became divine. He knew that God is, not as a person but as a quality.

It is as when the sun rises – the same quality. It is as when the cuckoo starts calling from the distance – the same quality. It is there in a roseflower. It is in the eyes of two lovers. It is there when a dancer loses himself in the dance, when the dancer disappears and only the dance remains.

DAY 13

My whole approach is not that of teaching you a certain belief, but of creating the right climate inside you. Bliss is the right climate.

Love, sing, dance, enjoy as much as you can. Everything that is possible to enjoy has to be enjoyed and only then, when you are rising higher and higher in your cheerfulness, does a sense of gratitude arise. At a certain point you start feeling the grace of God, the blessing of being here. Then there is gratitude – and that gratitude becomes worship.

DAY 14

The body is born and the body dies; the mind is born and the mind dies. But you are neither the body nor the mind. You are something transcendental to both, something that never dies and is never born. You have always been here and will always be here.

The moment one starts feeling it, the whole perspective on life starts changing. Whatever has been important up to that moment becomes unimportant: money, power, prestige, and all that.

And whatever has never been important before suddenly gains great importance: love, compassion, meditation, prayer, godliness.

Remember that within you there is something eternal.

DAY 15

Jesus says that the Kingdom of God is within you. That is the essential teaching of all the awakened ones: don't go anywhere; don't seek and search outside yourself, you will not find anything there. You will remain empty, unfulfilled, frustrated because the real kingdom – the real riches – are part of your interiority, of your subjectivity, of your soul.

Ordinary humanity is extrovert. That's exactly the meaning of the worldly man: extrovert. By becoming a sannyasin you will be moving in exactly the opposite direction: it is introversion.

Not that I am against the world, but not to know oneself is very dangerous. Once you know yourself you can roam all over the world sharing your joy and living your joy: then there is no problem. If you are rooted in your being, you can be as extrovert as you want, nothing can harm you. You can live in the marketplace, but your meditation will remain undisturbed.

But the first, the foremost thing is to settle within, to be acquainted with your inner reality. And my whole effort is to turn you in, in every possible way, to help you to go in. I cannot give you the truth, nobody can, but I can indicate where it is to be found. It is not to be found on the moon, it is not to be found on Everest; it is to be found just within you. Learn to close your eyes and see within.

DAY 16

Godliness is our substance, our very being. It is not something outside us, it is our innermost core, our interiority. We are not to seek and search for it. It has only to be remembered: we have forgotten it. Our godliness is not lost, it is just that we have forgotten who we are.

DAY 17

Man is capable of becoming a host to God, a home to God. And unless one becomes a host and a home to God, one remains unfulfilled. Without allowing God in, one remains in a deep frustration, because the moment God enters our being, we become God.

That is our ultimate destiny. And only when this destiny is fulfilled is there contentment and the joy of arriving.

DAY 18

We are very close to godliness, but like parallel lines we go on, never meeting. Once we stop going into the past and the future, the parallel lines start coming closer and closer together. One day, suddenly, there is only one line: the two lines have disappeared. That is the moment of great joy, great benediction. That's what everyone is seeking, longing for. And because people go on missing it, they become miserable. Be ready. And the only way to be ready is to live in the present, and you will become a home for godliness. That is the fulfillment of life.

DAY 19

Existence is our only security. Money power, prestige – nothing is secure. Family, friends, even life itself – nothing is secure. We are surrounded by insecurity.

There is one thing which is secure, and that one thing cannot be found anywhere outside. That one thing can only be found at our innermost core. God resides there. That is God's dwelling place – the heart of your hearts.

To know the God within is to go beyond all security. Then everything is safe and secure. And when everything is safe and secure, misery disappears naturally, anxiety disappears, and great bliss arises. That bliss is the deepest longing of your being.

DAY 20

There is only one secret worth knowing, that is your own innermost self. That is the secret-most place. People go on traveling far and wide; that is not difficult. Man has reached the moon – it is so easy. But it is very difficult to reach one's own center – and the secret of secrets is hidden there, the master key which can unlock all the mysteries.

DAY 21

The first thing to remember is that life has been given to us, it is not our achievement. In fact we don't deserve it at all. It is a very strange law of existence that those who deserve it – a Buddha, a Christ – disappear from life, and those who don't deserve it go on getting life again and again. Once you deserve it, you are ready to disappear into the ultimate. If you don't deserve it, you will have to come back. Only those who fail, come back – obviously. Those who fail have to come back to the same class, to the same school again. Those who pass, move to higher planes of being, to higher schools that are not ordinarily visible. This is the first thing to remember, that life is a gift. Don't waste it, use it. Use it in deserving it.

And the second thing to remember is strength of spirit. It is not something that is yours either, it is the constant flow of existence in you.

You are breathing it every moment, unconsciously of course. The moment you become conscious, you will be surprised. We eat existence, we breathe existence – there is nothing else but existence. It is our nourishment. It is our roots, it is our branches, the foliage, the flowers, the fruit. It is all and we are nothing.

DAY 22

The most difficult thing in life is to receive a gift because it goes against the ego. It is easier to give, very easy to give. But to receive is very difficult. And to receive when you don't deserve – then it becomes even more difficult. And we don't deserve – we have not earned it. We are not worthy of bliss, but existence goes on giving it; not because we deserve, but because it has it in such abundance. The moment you receive its bliss, it feels thankful to you. You have unburdened it, you have taken a little weight from its being. But remember, it is very difficult to receive a gift. It feels like a humiliation. One feels a little embarrassed. A sannyasin has to learn how to receive a gift in great joy and celebration because the more receptive you become, the more will be given to you. If you are totally receptive, the whole of heaven can descend into your being this very moment, here now. All that is needed on your part is to be absolutely open and ready.

DAY 23

All the masters of all the ages have declared that everybody is born a divine king but is utterly unaware of the fact. Not knowing our own inner world, we remain unaware of our kingdom. And because we are unaware of the kingdom that belongs to us, that is forever ours, we go on desiring small things, begging for small things.

We are dreaming that we are beggars. The moment one wakes up, one is in for a great surprise: one finds one is not a beggar, one is a king.

That's the whole purpose of meditation – to make you aware of your kingdom, to make you aware of your highest potential. And once you start becoming aware, then the journey is not difficult. Just a little awakening and the sleep is almost gone, then things become easier.

DAY 24

Once you are aware, you start seeking and searching for a second birth. And the second birth becomes possible only through meditation. The first birth is through the mother, the second birth is through meditation: hence in ancient scriptures, meditation is called the real mother.

Jesus says to his disciples, "Unless you are born again you will not enter the Kingdom of God." In the East, the person who has attained to God is called *dwija*, twice born. The second birth releases the fragrance.

DAY 25

Western meditation is nothing but a kind of thinking. Thinking of higher things is called meditation. When you think of God, when you think of Christ, when you think of love, it is called meditation.

In the East, thinking is not meditation at all. Whether you think of God or of money doesn't matter; any thinking of any object is a disturbance in meditation. In the East, meditation means a state of no thought, just pure being. And that is the greatest experience in life – when you simply exist. No thought crosses your being. All the traffic stops, the mind disappears. But consciousness is there, more than ever, because whatever was hidden behind the thoughts is no longer hidden. Whatever was involved in thoughts is no longer involved. All the energy is released. One is simply a pool of energy, and so silent that not even a ripple arises. In that silent pool of consciousness, of energy, existence is reflected; we come to know that which is. Godliness is another name for that which is.

DAY 26

The only preparation required to experience godliness is to put the mind aside. That's what meditation is all about – a strategy to stop this constantly chattering mind, this crazy mind that goes on and on for no reason at all. It is busy without any business. I am not saying that the mind has to be destroyed; it has only to be put aside so when you need it you can use it. It is like your car parked in the garage. When you want to use it you can take it out of the garage, then you are the master.

But ordinarily the situation has become just the reverse: the car insists on not going into the garage. The car says, "I am not going to stop." The car says, "You have to run with me." And it goes on running, twenty-four hours a day. Even while you are asleep the mind goes on and on. Ordinarily, once it starts in childhood it never stops until death, unless somebody starts moving into meditation.

For the very few who enter meditation, mind stops and suddenly they become aware of the sun that was hiding behind the clouds of the mind. That awareness of the ultimate light, of the ultimate sun, is divine knowledge.

DAY 27

We live on the periphery, we live in the mind, and the mind is so noisy that it does not allow us to hear the still, small voice within. A master is needed only as a device because you know how to hear the outside. The master says from the outside what existence has been trying to tell you from the inside for centuries. But you don't listen to the inner.

Listening to the inner master, slowly, slowly one becomes conscious: "What is happening?" The master is saying the same things that somehow you feel to be your own, more your own than your mind, more your own than your body. That's why the East calls the master a God. The West is absolutely unable to understand the phenomenon. The East knows why the master is called a God: he represents God, he reflects God because he reflects your reality, your true being.

Being with a master is simply getting ready to turn in one day, so that you can close your eyes and look in, so that you can start hearing what your own intuition goes on telling you. And the intuition is always right. The intellect may be right, may be wrong. It is always either–or; doubt persists, it is never indubitable. But intuition is without any doubt, it simply knows. The intuitive person never repents because he never does anything wrong. He cannot. He simply follows the voice of existence within.

DAY 28

Meditation means awareness, alertness, watchfulness, witnessing. Witness your actions, witness your thoughts, witness your feelings, so that slowly, slowly you can see you are neither the body nor the mind nor the heart – you are the witness of it all.

The moment you know that you are only a witness, a pure mirror reflecting everything, and you are not identified with any reflection, suddenly you discover your inner light. It is already there, but we have to shift our consciousness. A one-hundred-and-eighty-degree turn is needed, and it happens only by witnessing, there is no other method. When you are witnessing, one thing becomes clear: you are not the thing that you are witnessing, obviously; you are the witness of it.

Go on, deeper and deeper. When nothing is left to witness, you have witnessed all objects that you can witness and you have rejected them knowing "I am not that," when everything is eliminated, only you are left – just the mirror and nothing else – suddenly the shift: consciousness turns upon itself.

That moment of turning in is the greatest moment in life. In that very moment you know who you are and you know what God is, and you know what bliss is, you know what truth is, freedom is, what eternity is. All that is worth knowing is known – immediately, instantly. And then you can go on living in the world but you will be living with a totally different center, with a totally different perspective: you will be in the world, but absolutely out of the world.

DAY 29

What is courage? The most significant definition is the capacity to drop the familiar, the known, because that's what mind is – the familiar, the known, the past. And the moment you drop the past, you open up to infinities. But man is afraid to be so open, man feels lost in that vast space.

Mind is a small thing. It feels cozy, warm. It is like a golden cage. It is beautiful, you can decorate it – and everybody tries to decorate it. That's what our education is for: to decorate the golden cage and make it so beautiful that it becomes almost impossible for you to leave it. You start clinging to it. You forget that you have wings, that the whole sky is a challenge, that you have to go to the stars, that there is a long, long journey ahead.

Hence, my definition of courage is the capacity to drop the

golden cage of the mind and to go into the unknown, in spite of all the fears, in spite of the insecurity of it all. Only the person who has that quality is religious.

DAY 30

Life is synonymous with God. God is not the creator of life, but life itself: he is not separate from life. The very idea of the creator is false. He is not like a painter, because the painter is separate from the painting. He is more like a dancer; he remains one with it. Hence, one need not go to a temple, to a mosque, to a synagogue to worship God. Life is more than is needed. This whole earth, this whole existence, is full of God, over-flowing with God. He is the green and the red and the gold of the trees. He is all over the place: you cannot avoid him. We collide with him every moment.

It is just because we have some idea of God that we go on missing him. We have some idea that he is somewhere far away in heaven: hence we go on missing him. Drop that stupid idea and you will find him everywhere. He is very close by. Once, Ramakrishna was asked, "Where is God?" And he said, "Tell me where he is not. I have been searching for a place where he is not and I have failed. I have not yet found a place where he is not."

DAY 31

To be a friend to existence means saying yes to existence, yes in all its moods. Sometimes it is cloudy – still the yes is there. Sometimes it is very sunny, and sometimes a dark moment arrives – misery surrounds you, or anger or rage – still you say yes deep down because whatsoever life is, is divine. In its totality it is divine.

DAY 32

Everything is a gift from existence. We don't deserve anything, we are not worthy of anything. Existence gives us life, the capacity to love, the capacity to feel beauty, the capacity to find truth – not because we are worthy, not because we deserve them, but because it has too much.

It is like a cloud full of rain: it has to shower. It is out of its abundance that we receive. It is like a flower that has inexhaustible perfume – it is bound to be released to the winds. It is like a light – beginningless, endless. It has to be shared; otherwise it becomes a burden.

DAY 33

Life is a gift, birth is a gift, love is a gift, death is a gift. If we know how to appreciate, all is a gift; if we don't know how to appreciate, there is nothing but complaints and complaints in life.

There are only two types of people. Those who know how to appreciate the beauty of that which is, of that which has been given to them, and those who have no sense of appreciation: they are always condemning, complaining, asking for more and more.

Only the first kind of people can become religious, the second kind cannot become religious. The second kind is bound to deny God sooner or later, because God becomes an enemy who is not fulfilling your desires. It is those people who have made the proverb: "Man proposes and God disposes."

The proverb is made by nonreligious people. They are always feeling frustrated, whatever happens is wrong. It is never up to the mark, it is never fulfilling, never to their heart's content; it is always falling short. They live in misery because there is always a grudge, as if they are deprived of something.

How can they feel grateful? And without gratefulness there is no prayer, without prayer there is no religion.

DAY 34

Prayer is praising existence for all that is. It is the approach of a yes-saying heart which knows no doubt, no skepticism, no negativity, which can dance and sing because the world is so beautiful. It is such a gift, of which we are not worthy. We cannot repay existence; all that we can do is praise. We can sing hallelujah! And if one becomes a full hallelujah, nothing else is needed. Then everything is possible, then even the impossible is possible.

So let prayer be your path. Praise in as many ways as possible and never complain. Drop the complaining mind. And it is only a question of decision. Once it is decided, one starts dropping the old habit of complaining and all the energy starts moving in praise. Praise brings blessings, benediction.

Praise in all possible ways: praise the sunset, and the clouds, and the trees, and the birds and the people. Don't be a miser in praising. Praise wholeheartedly, as totally as possible, and it will bring you closer and closer to existence. It will become the bridge. It is the shortest route to existence. Meditation is a long route, prayer is a shortcut.

DAY 35

Prayer is the foundation of religion, and it is prayer realized that becomes the experience of godliness. The seed of prayer is gratitude.

Feel grateful because great are the gifts of existence and it is constantly showering on you, but we start taking it for granted. That is one of the most stupid things that a human being can do, but the mind is always doing it: it starts taking things for granted. The sun rises, the dawn has tremendous beauty, but your mind says, "So what? It happens every day. It is just another morning, just like others." The whole of the east is red with the rising sun and the clouds are full of color, but the mind says, "So what? It is nothing new. It has happened millions of times and it is going to happen again millions of times."

If this is the way of looking at things – and this *is* how mind looks at things, it becomes insensitive: insensitive to beauty, insensitive to music, insensitive to poetry, insensitive to love, insensitive to everything that is valuable. Then naturally you live in darkness, you live in ugliness. It is your own creation.

DAY 36

Just dissolve yourself into a loving energy, just become a loving energy – not in love with something in particular, but just having love for each and everything, even for nothing! It is not a question of an object for love, but just of an overflowing loving energy.

If you are sitting silently in your room, let the room be full of loving energy, create an aura of love around yourself. And you *can* do it, that's why I am saying it. I only give things to you which I can see are possible. I don't ask the impossible – never! I only indicate what is going to happen to you very naturally. It is very simple and very naturally possible for you to become just love. That will be your prayer and that will be your meditation.

If you are looking at the trees, you are in love with the trees. If you are looking at the stars, you are in love with the stars. You are love, that's all. So wherever you are, go on pouring your love. And when you pour love on rocks, even rocks are no longer rocks. Love is such a miracle, such magic, that it transforms everything into the beloved. You become love and existence becomes your beloved, existence becomes God. People seek and search for God without becoming love. How can they find him? They don't have the necessary equipment, the necessary context and space.

Create love and forget all about God. Suddenly one day you will encounter him everywhere.

DAY 37

Be as silent as possible. Sit more and more in stillness – not only in bodily stillness. That too is helpful and creates a situation, but it is not the end, it is just the beginning. It is more important that the mind should be still, that the mind should stop its constant chattering. And it does stop – we have just never tried.

All that is needed is a very simple process: sit inside yourself and watch. Let the mind do all kinds of old tricks and you simply watch nonjudgmentally, neither saying good nor bad, neither choosing nor rejecting – utterly indifferent, cool. Slowly, slowly the knack is learned by remaining cool and indifferent. First the mind tries all its old tricks, and then by and by it starts feeling embarrassed because you are not getting affected in any way, this way or that. Even if you become affected against it, the mind is perfectly at ease: it has disturbed you. So don't be against it, don't fight with it, and don't fall a victim to its tricks. Just remain aloof.

Many times you will get involved; the moment you remember, pull yourself out. Again compose yourself, again start watching.

A thought arises – see it. It comes in front of you – see it. Then it passes by. Take note of it, with no idea of whether it is good or bad, whether it should be or should not be, with no moral attitude, just a scientific, cool observation. Within three to nine months, the mind stops chattering.

One day, suddenly it is not there, and that day such a silence descends as you have never known before. Then it never leaves you: it remains with you, becomes your very soul. It is liberating.

DAY 38

Be more and more silent. Whenever you have the opportunity, just sit silently doing nothing, not even meditation. Just sit silently for no reason, for no purpose. Slowly, slowly silence grows, it becomes an overwhelming experience. And when silence has permeated you through and through, you will know who you are and you will know what this life is all about. In knowing it, one knows godliness.

DAY 39

Before death comes, attain something of eternity, have a taste of something which is timeless, deathless; then death cannot destroy you. Then you can die dancing, singing, laughing. And to be able to die singing, laughing, dancing, is the greatest achievement of life.

DAY 40

The door to the divine is spontaneity. To be spontaneous is to be in godliness. Mind is never spontaneous. It is either in the past or in the future, either in that which is no more or in that which is not yet. Between these two it goes on missing that which is, and that is the door. The present moment is not part of time; hence the present moment is not available to the mind. Mind and time are synonymous. You can say that mind is time inside your being, and time is mind outside you, but they are one phenomenon. The present moment is neither part of time nor part of the mind. When you are in the present moment, you are in godliness. That is the true meaning of meditation, the true meaning of prayer, the true meaning of love. And when one acts out of the present moment, that action is never binding because it is not your action, it is godliness acting through you. It is godliness flowing through you.

DAY 41

Drop all boundaries, become infinite. Think only in terms of infinity, eternity. Less than that has never satisfied anybody and is not going to satisfy anybody – ever.

The boundary of the body has to be dropped. We are too identified with our bodies. We think that we are the body, and we are not. This is the first falsehood that has to be dropped. Out of this falsehood many other falsehoods arise. If one is identified with the body, one will be afraid of old age, disease, death. They grow out of this identification with the body.

Think of yourself as pure consciousness. You are not the body, you are the one who is aware of the body. And you are not the mind either.

First start working with the body because it is easier to start with the gross. Then move to the subtle; look at the mind as separate from yourself. As you become aware that you are neither the body nor the mind, you will feel great freedom arising in you, unhindered.

There will be no obstruction, no walls, but in all directions open space. Then the most subtle barrier has to be dropped – that of feeling.

That is the subtlest. First body, then mind, then heart; and to be free from the heart is to be enlightened.

DAY 42

We are all strangers here. This is not our home, our home is somewhere else. We are in a foreign land. To remain outside oneself is to remain homeless; to come in is to be back home. Now every effort has to be made to come in. No stone is to be left unturned. Everything has to be risked because nothing is more precious than this turning in. Everything can be lost for it, sacrificed for it because all else is trivia.

DAY 43

The religious person lives egolessly. He knows: "I am part of the whole, an intrinsic part of the whole, not at all separate." To know that you are not separate from the whole brings tremendous freedom. It brings vastness, the whole sky is yours. You are no longer identified with a small, very small ego. We are vast, but we have become confined in small spaces; that's why there is so much misery. It is like forcing an ocean into a dewdrop. We are birds with wings that need to have the whole sky, but are encaged. Nobody is encaging us, but the irony is we go on encaging ourselves. We are the prison, and we are the prisoner and we are the jailer – there is nobody else. That's why the mystics call it a dream – it is a dream. The moment you wake up, you find: "This is strange. I was chased by a lion, but I was the lion and I was chased. And I was the spectator too, the witness to the whole thing!" This is how life is, like a dream.

Now it is time… If children play with stupid games, they can be forgiven. They need to go astray, they need to commit many mistakes. But as you grow older you cannot be forgiven.

And the ego is the most stupid game because it is against reality, it is against existence. Sannyas simply means becoming aware of the fact that the ego is a false entity, our own creation, our own projection, and that we are caught in it. It is like a spider's web: the spider creates the web from inside of itself. We go on creating our own prisons out of our imagination, our desire, our memory, our ambition, our jealousy. And they all go on spinning subtle structures around us. The whole structure is called the ego; the whole work of the mind is called the ego. From this very moment, become aware of it and slowly, slowly get out of it.

DAY 44

Ego is our hell and the irony is that we are the creators of it. We create it and we suffer. But it is within our capacity not to create it and to move away from suffering. The moment the ego is not there and the suffering is not there, you are in bliss.

Bliss is our nature; suffering is a created phenomenon, arbitrary. Bliss is uncreated: it is there right now, underneath suffering, like an undercurrent. You need not create it, it is already the case – just don't create suffering.

DAY 45

Ego consists of feeling and thinking that we are separate from existence, that we are like islands. That is absolutely false. We don't exist in separation, we can't exist even for a single moment in separation. The breath that comes in keeps us joined with the outside. And we are not only breathing with the nose, we are breathing through every pore of the body. We are thirsty – we drink water and the water quenches the thirst. It is continuously moving from the outer toward the inner and from the inner toward the outer. Food is continuously in circulation, breath is in circulation. We are in constant exchange with reality. We are not separate; we are bridged in a thousand and one ways.

DAY 46

The ego can exist only if you fight. Surrender is poison to the ego, hence the emphasis on surrender. Fight is food to the ego, surrender is poison.

And the ego has to die, only then can you be born. In one sheath there can't be two swords. Either you can live inside yourself and the ego goes, or the ego lives and you have to go underground. That's how millions of people are – living underground lives and the egos are sitting on the throne. In surrender, the ego disappears and your underground self starts surfacing, back to its natural status, its natural state. Your life can be an instrument of existence, a bamboo flute on its lips. You just have to be hollow and let it sing the song if it wants. Or if it does not want, then silence is as beautiful as a song.

DAY 47

The man who has never known anything of meditation lives a barren life, just like a desert.

I have heard about an American tourist dressed in his swim-suit running toward the ocean, perspiring. He met a man and he asked, "How far is the ocean?"

The man looked at the American, felt very sorry for him and said, "It will be difficult to reach it – this is the Sahara and the ocean is at least eight hundred miles away from here." The American said, "Then I will have to rest here on the beach!"

You can believe your desert to be a beach. That's how people are living, believing their desert is a beach. It is simply a desert. At least in the Sahara, after eight hundred miles, you will find the ocean, but in a life without meditation, the Sahara is unending. Not even after eight hundred miles…

DAY 48

Bliss is never our achievement. It cannot be because it happens only when we have disappeared. If we are still there to claim that we have achieved it, it is pseudo bliss, it is not true, it is just a dream; soon it will be gone and you will fall back into misery. Mind has played a trick on you – and mind is very cunning, very political, very diplomatic. It goes on finding ways and means to keep you hanging around it. And the ultimate trick, the last trick that it can play is to create a false sense of bliss.

Real bliss is always a gift from existence, and it can happen only when the ego dies. The ego is the barrier. The moment you are not, existence is, and the experience of existence happening in your total silence and nothingness is bliss. That dance of existence in your absolutely silent space, with nothing to interfere – no mind, no ego to distort it, to hamper it, to hinder it – that is bliss.

The work of meditation is negative; it is to destroy the ego. Then bliss comes on its own.

DAY 49

Meditation means becoming silent, still, thoughtless, but fully aware. Meditation can be reduced to a small definition: no mind and all awareness.

Right now there is no awareness and all mind. Right now one hundred percent is mind and zero percent is awareness. We have to change the whole phenomenon: we have to bring awareness to one hundred percent and mind to zero percent. Then one becomes an emperor. Then you know that this whole existence is yours, that all the stars are yours. Then there is no need to possess anything, it is already yours. There is no need to desire anything, it is already given to you.

The whole of existence is given to you as a gift, but we have not been able to recognize it yet. We have not yet been able to see what has been given to us: the life, the love, the joy. We are concerned about small, mundane things and wasting our time, life, energy.

Meditation brings into focus the reality of who you are and what you really possess. Knowing it, all misery, all anxiety disappears. Knowing it, one is freed from all darkness, one becomes light itself.

DAY 50

Meditate so that prayer can happen. And the only proof that prayer has happened is that you will experience the fragrance, and others will experience the fragrance of your experience. You will radiate it. You will *be* it, and whatever you touch will start dancing with joy. Even dust is transformed into gold by the touch of a man who knows what prayer is.

Prayer is sheer magic – but it comes out of meditation, never otherwise. Hence, my insistence is on meditation, not on prayer, because I know prayer is inevitable. If meditation happens, prayer is inevitable. If prayer is there, fragrance is a natural consequence.

So I don't teach prayer, I don't teach service to humanity because I know that meditation is all that is needed. Once meditation is there, everything follows in its own time, in the right time. Prayer comes, and out of prayer, service to humanity – that's its fragrance.

DAY 51

A prayer without meditation is false because it depends on beliefs; you have to believe in a God you don't know. How can you really pray to a God you don't know? You can deceive others and yourself, but prayer cannot arise out of belief; that would be basically dishonest. And if even prayer is dishonest, what can be honest in life?

But there are millions of people in the world who know nothing of meditation and still go on praying. They are carrying plastic flowers believing that they are real roses. Hence they go on praying but their lives have no fragrance of prayer. On the contrary, their lives stink of all kinds of jealousies, hatreds, violence, greed. There seems to be no fragrance at all.

My own observation is that real religion begins in meditation. Meditation means a state of thoughtless silence. And when you are absolutely silent with no thought disturbing your silence, stirring it, the joy of such a silence is so tremendous that you are bound to thank the universe. It is impossible not to, it is impossible not to feel grateful. It is not a question of belief anymore: you know the bliss, you have experienced the silence, the music of it. And out of the music your heart is full of prayerfulness. You bow to existence.

DAY 52

Prayer is nothing but silence, pure silence. You are not saying anything to anybody; the other is absolutely absent. There is no content in your consciousness, not even a small ripple in the lake of consciousness: all is still and silent.

Nothing is said, but the beat of the heart, the flow of the blood, the very grace that surrounds that silence is prayer – and a tremendous feeling to bow down to the whole of existence for all that it has done for us.

Hence I don't teach prayer here, I only teach silence; prayer is a necessary outcome of silence, is a flowering of silence. You work to create silence and when your work is complete, prayer arrives. It is just like spring coming and the trees are full of flowers. Create silence and you have created the spring. Now the flowers are not far away, they are bound to come. It is part of the ultimate law – *aes dhammo sanantano*. These are Buddha's words. This is the law, the ultimate law: create silence and you will be blessed by prayer.

DAY 53

Bliss is beloved of all. Whatever we are doing, we are searching for bliss. In every act – right or wrong, moral or immoral, material or spiritual – the search is the same, the search for the ultimate beloved. And that is bliss. If one searches for bliss unconsciously, one cannot find it. That's how many people go on searching and searching, and they always find only misery. And the more they reach, the more miserable they become. But the reason is that their search is unconscious. They have not yet become alert to what they are really seeking and searching for.

The moment you become aware that bliss is our goal, things become simple. God is not your goal, truth is not your goal. These are different names which you go on giving to bliss. All these names have to be removed so that you can face the ultimate goal in its sheer nakedness – because once you know what the goal is, things become simple. Once you know the goal, immediately you know the path; once you recognize that bliss is our goal, you need not go outside at all because bliss is our very nature. The way is in, not out. You have not to rush and run for it. You have to be more still and more silent.

And the moment that you are totally still and silent, it wells up within your being.

DAY 54

A man of awareness, a meditative person, is never distracted because he watches everything. He will watch the phone ringing, he will watch the child crying, he will watch the neighbors and their radio getting louder and louder – he has nothing to do with it. He is cool and calm and open from all sides. So whatever happens – the train whistles, the airplane passes by, or there is a distant call of the cuckoo – everything is included. Concentration means only one thing is included, everything else is excluded. Meditation means all is included, nothing is excluded; you are simply resting within yourself.

It is a knack. If you go on doing it, slowly, slowly the knack is learned. And the moment you have learned the knack of meditation you are a new being. It is a new birth, the real birth, because in that very moment you know you are neither the body nor the mind, you are pure consciousness. In that very moment, you know that this pure consciousness was before birth, and is going to remain after death.

It is immortal. This is the discovery of immortality. And to discover immortality is to discover godliness, to discover immortality is to discover eternity.

DAY 55

Learn how to disappear, how to evaporate. Learn how not to be. That is the greatest art in life because the ego is so cunning; it always finds some way to come in from the back door. It can become humble, it can become pious, it can become saintly, it can become holy. It can play all kinds of games. A sannyasin has to be constantly alert not to allow the ego to play any more games.

Be watchful. And the more you know the ways of the ego, the more you are free of it because it can no longer play upon you whatever strategy you have come to know. Slowly, slowly all doors are closed. One day, when the last strategy has collapsed, you are freed from yourself.

That is liberation. And that is the ultimate goal of all religious effort. Only in that liberated state can one know what truth is.

DAY 56

Make it a point now to give more and more emphasis to the inner, more and more time and space to the inner. And it is only a question of remembering.

Slowly, slowly your consciousness takes a turn. And when you start facing yourself, you are facing the greatest phenomenon, the most exquisite, the most beautiful experience of life because you are seeing life in its intrinsic grace and splendor.

DAY 57

Man is born with a very small flame of godliness within him, but it is hidden behind layers and layers of darkness. So whenever one enters oneself, first one has to pass through a jungle of darkness – and that's what scares many people. Many people try to go in, but then they escape again because that darkness makes them very afraid. It looks like death.

The Christian mystics have given it the right name: the dark night of the soul. But one has to pass through the dark night, otherwise there is no dawn. The dark night is the womb for the dawn. The master is needed to help you while you are passing through the darkness.

Once you have seen your own light there is no need for any help. You are grateful to the master, but you have come home, the journey is over.

DAY 58

Whenever you have time, forget the outer; it is superficial. Dive deep into the inner, and you will find the light, the light that is our very life, the light that is the stuff we are made of and of which the whole universe is also made.

In the old days that stuff was called God. Now that word has become a little dangerous. People don't like that word; it looks a little old-fashioned. It smells of priesthood, churches, and the smell is not good.

So I don't say you will encounter God within. But I can't help it, you will. That light is what God is. And unless you know that you are something eternal which cannot be destroyed by anything, you remain on the circumference, accidental.

DAY 59

Religion is nothing but the simple art of dissolving yourself into the whole. The whole is called God. That's why the man who has attained to God is called holy. He has become whole, he is no longer separate; he has dropped that stupid idea of being separate. He is no longer like an ice cube, he has melted and merged into the ocean.

That moment is the moment of great bliss. And after that one can never fall from bliss – there is no way to fall. Even if one wants to be miserable, one cannot be.

The ordinary person who lives like an ego tries hard to be blissful but he cannot be, he remains miserable. And the surrendered person, even if he tries to be miserable, cannot be. Bliss is the consequence of surrender; and misery the consequence of resistance.

DAY 60

Once your inner light is found, your life is nothing but pure bliss. It is not only bliss for you, it becomes contagious, it starts affecting other people. Those who are receptive will start feeling something when they are close to you. Their hearts will respond, some bells will start ringing in their beings – a kind of synchronicity.

One man becoming blissful can trigger a process in thousands of people. Hence my interest is not in society, but in individuals. If I can transform a few thousand people, that will do – they will ignite thousands more. And it is an unending process, it goes on and on.

DAY 61

Man is not as small as he appears from the outside. He contains the whole sky within, he contains all the oceans. Yes, he looks like a dewdrop, but his appearance is very deceptive. And science is still working on his appearance, the dewdrop.

Those who have penetrated deeper into human consciousness were surprised to find that as you go deeper, man becomes vast. When you reach his very core, he is the whole universe. And that is the experience of godliness. Meditate and go deeper inward. It is already there – we just have to uncover it.

DAY 62

Anything that brings you bliss is nourishment to the soul. And it is not only that people's bodies are starving, their souls are starving far more.

So from this moment, be alert: choose bliss as much as possible. Avoid misery; never cooperate with any misery that at times surrounds you. It's bound to surround you, just like clouds come one day and another day it is sunny. Watch the clouds, watch the sun, and remember that you are separate from both. Dark moments come, light moments come – we are moving on a wheel of day and night, birth and death, summer and winter. But if we can remember that we are none of these, bliss arises. Then one is suddenly at peace with oneself and at peace with existence. That is bliss – that harmony, that accord, that attunement.

And once you have learned to be blissful, your soul starts growing. Otherwise it remains a seed, it never becomes a tree. And unless the seed becomes a tree and the tree blooms and brings much fruit, life is a waste.

DAY 63

A miserable person, knowingly or unknowingly, goes on creating misery for others. He cannot help it; he can give only that which he has. Even if he does not want to bring misery to others, he is a victim of his own misery. Even if he wants to do some good, the ultimate result is going to be bad. In spite of all his good intentions, his actions will bring misery to people because nothing can arise out of a miserable person that can bring bliss to people. That's the very definition of good, virtue: helping people to be blissful. But you can give only that which you have; hence to me, bliss is virtue, the only virtue.

Be blissful – that's what I teach. I don't teach you to be virtuous because that is secondary, that is a by-product. I teach the real transformation within you. Move from misery to bliss and then whatsoever you do will be good; it cannot be anything else.

DAY 64

Bliss is only for those who are courageous, daring, brave, because bliss happens only when you have moved beyond the known into the unknown. Whenever you are confined to the known, your life becomes routine, repetitive. It goes on moving in the same rut, it goes around in circles, and slowly, slowly it dulls all your sensitivity, all your receptivity.

It hardens people. It makes them blind, it makes them deaf, it makes them dumb, because there is nothing to see and nothing to hear and nothing to taste and nothing to feel. They have known it all; it is the same repetition. How can there be bliss in such a life? Such a life has only one taste – that of misery, depression, sadness, a settled sadness. But if one is courageous enough to move continuously from the known into the unknown, from the familiar into the unfamiliar…

It is risky because the familiar is secure, safe. And who knows what is going to happen if you go into the unknown, into the uncharted? You take your small boat and you go into the uncharted sea. Who knows if you will ever come back to the old shore again? Who can give you a guarantee? There is no guarantee. But unless one is ready to live in such a dangerous state, one cannot remain blissful. Live dangerously because life knows no other way: it has to be lived dangerously. Remember that as one of the most fundamental qualities of a religious life – partic-ularly the way I see religion.

DAY 65

The greatest courage in the world is to not imitate others, to live one's own life as authentically as possible, whatever the cost. Even if life is lost in living your own life, it is worth it because that is how the soul is born. When one is ready to die for something, in that very agony – the word *agony* means struggle – in that very struggle one is born, it is a birth pain. It takes courage, it takes guts.

Live your life without being bothered by the moralists, puritans, priests, stupid people who go on giving advice. Live your life. Even if you live in error, then too it is better to live your own life than to be right according to somebody else; the man who is right according to somebody else is false, and the man who is wrong out of his own decision is going to learn from his error sooner or later. He will grow out of it, he will be benefited by it. The only person who learns is the person who is ready to commit errors and the best way to commit errors is not to listen to others – just go on doing your thing!

DAY 66

Life is for the courageous. The coward only vegetates. The coward goes on hesitating, and by the time he decides, the moment is lost. The coward only thinks to live but never lives, thinks to love but never loves. And the world is full of cowards. The coward has a basic fear, the fear of the unknown. He keeps himself within the boundaries of the known, of the familiar. Courage begins when you step beyond the boundaries of the known. It is risky – it is dangerous. But the more you risk, the more you are. The more you accept the challenge of the unknown, the more integrated you become. It is only in tremendous danger that the soul is born; otherwise the person remains just the body. For millions of people the soul is only a possibility, not a reality. Only a very few courageous ones have been full of soul.

DAY 67

The two qualities of being courageous and being blissful prepare the ground for God to descend in you. You have to be courageous because godliness is unknown. Whatever you have heard about God, when you really come to know him you will be surprised. All that you heard about him was sheer nonsense, bullshit! There is no way to describe the experience. Godliness remains indefinable, inexpressible. It is so unknown, even those who have experienced it cannot relate their experience to anybody else; one simply remains dumb. The English word *mystic* is very beautiful. Its original meaning is: one who has become dumb through experiencing, one who has come across such a truth that he can only say it is mysterious, that it is a mystery – which is saying nothing.

DAY 68

When you are climbing toward the heights, reaching toward God – because that is the only true height, everything else is far below – when you are trying to reach toward God, you become the ascending one. And the miracle is that when you start ascending toward God, God starts descending toward you.

The meeting always happens somewhere in between, it is not one way. It is not only that the seeker moves toward God, the moment the seeker starts moving, God starts moving; it is simultaneous. It is in fact two polarities of one process – the seeker and the sought; it is one phenomenon. But God cannot descend in you unless you start ascending.

People go on living as if this mundane life is all there is. People go on living as if there is nothing higher possible. There is immense possibility. Man comes with a great potential. The ultimate height of every man's being is godliness.

DAY 69

Before bliss can happen, you have to become integrated like a rock. People are like sand, just thousands of fragments, a crowd, a multitude: they are not one. And bliss can happen only when you are one; otherwise your inner crowd will go on creating noise, conflict, struggle, tension, anguish.

The whole crowd has to be melted into one unity. When that integration happens, bliss naturally comes as a by-product. Bliss is a by-product of inner integrity, and the rock represents integration.

DAY 70

The whole of existence is surrounded by a divine energy that protects you, cares for you, is always available. If you go on missing it, it is only because of you. If you keep your doors closed, the sun may be outside but you will live in darkness. Even if the doors are open and the sun is there, you can keep your eyes closed and you will still live in darkness. So is the case with existence: its love is always there, but our hearts are not open, our hearts are closed. Sannyas means opening the heart. Make your heart available to existence so that you can receive, so that you can pulsate with the whole, in accord with the whole. And then great benediction is yours.

DAY 71

Meditators are bound to be more intelligent than other people. If they are not, then their meditation is false, then they don't know what meditation is; they are doing something else in the name of meditation.

A meditative person is bound to be more sensitive, more intelligent, more creative, more loving, more compassionate. These qualities grow of their own accord. And the whole secret is in one thing: learn to stop the mind. The moment you know how to stop the mind, you become the master, and then the mind is a beautiful mechanism. You use it when you want to use it, when it is needed, and you turn it off when it is not needed.

DAY 72

Become more and more conscious of all that you do, of all that you think, all that you desire, imagine, dream. Just remember that you have to be conscious of everything. Walking, be conscious of it; eating, be conscious of it; thinking, go on watching the thoughts passing in the mind. One day you will be surprised, when you have learned the knack of watching, it continues even in sleep. You go on watching the dreams. You know what kind of dreams are passing by, and you know that they are dreams. That day, when one can watch one's own dreams, is a day of great transformation. From that moment onward you are a new being. Then you enter the world of reality.

By watching dreams, thoughts, desires, slowly, slowly we become the watcher, we become disidentified with all that we are watching, we become the witness. And that witness is the ultimate reality.

DAY 73

If you look around at the so-called religious lives, one thing is certain: every religion has been destructive. It has hampered people, obstructed them, made them so afraid of everything that the small joys of life – even drinking tea – became a sin. Drinking water in the night becomes a sin. Once you start moving in the direction of making things into sins, you cannot live, you only drag.

My approach is totally different. There are mistakes, but there are no sins at all. There are errors but no sins. And one can commit errors because it is only through committing errors that one learns. Only one thing has to be remembered: don't commit the same error again and again because that is stupid. One should explore life, and in exploring, sometimes you go astray. If you are too afraid of going astray, you cannot explore. Then the whole adventure of life is crushed, killed, destroyed. And that's what so-called religious people have done: they have made religion so serious, so somber, they have given religion such a long face.

My effort is to give you joy, gusto for life, courage to be adventurous; to move fearlessly, exploring all the possibilities that life makes available, fearless in expanding and being open and vulnerable. Because God is our judge we need not be afraid. Finally at the judgment day when you see God, you can tell him, "Yes, I have been drinking… Please forgive me. I have tried a few other things also." And I think he will understand. Don't be worried!

DAY 74

It is hard to drop the old, but it has to be dropped because only then is the new possible. It is hard to accept the new because it is new and we are unfamiliar with it. It is a stranger, and deep down we are apprehensive and afraid. But one has to learn to love the new; otherwise no growth is possible. Growth simply means the courage to drop the old, and the courage to love the new. And this is not to be done only once, it has to be done every moment, because every moment something is becoming old and something new is knocking at the door. Whenever that is happening, listen to the new and become utterly deaf to the old.

The old functions as bondage, the new brings freedom. Truth is always new. Existence is always fresh, as fresh as the dewdrops in the early morning sun.

DAY 75

Truth is not available ready-made. It is neither in the traditions nor in the scriptures. It has to be inquired into, explored, and everyone has to inquire into it. I may have found it but I cannot give it to you. It is not that I don't want to give it to you, but it is nontransferable. It simply can't be given; there is no way to give it. The moment you give it, it becomes a lie. You have to discover it on your own.

Buddhas can show the way, but you will have to travel the whole journey. It is a long, arduous journey but tremendously beautiful. Each moment is full of surprise, each moment is so full of wonder.

DAY 76

Truth is available only to the innocent consciousness – a consciousness that is as innocent as a child, a consciousness that knows nothing. When you know, your mirror is full of dust – knowledge gathers dust like a mirror. When you don't know anything, you are full of wonder and awe, your mirror is clean. And that clean mirror reflects the truth.

DAY 77

Truth is not something that has to be achieved, it is already inside us. We are it – the seeker is the sought. But we go on rushing hither and thither searching for the truth. We will never find it anywhere else; hence the only way to find it is to stop seeking it outside. The only way to find it is to sit silently and look within. It is not a question of doing something, it is more a question of not doing anything.

When you are in a state of non-doing, utterly relaxed, it happens, it wells up. It has always been there, but you have never been there. The meeting happens when you are also inside yourself.

DAY 78

A lamp is burning within you. It has always been there; we just never look at it. We are keeping our back toward it; hence we live in darkness.

Darkness is our own creation. If we turn in, all is light; if we look out, all is dark. Darkness simply means that we have become focused on the outside and forgotten the inner world.

DAY 79

We are born of light, we live in light, we die in light – we are made out of light. This has been one of the greatest insights of the mystics of all the ages. The scientists have also agreed to it just now, within the last twenty years; they had to agree. Just twenty years ago they were laughing at the mystics, thinking that they were talking nonsense: "Man made of light? They must be talking metaphorically, not literally." But mystics were really talking literally.

Now science not only says that man is made of light, but that everything is made of light; all is made of electrons, electricity. Science has come to this understanding through a very, very long route. The objective route is a very long route; the subjective route is very easy, the shortest possible, because you have only to look within. Nothing else is required: no lab, no instruments, no sophisticated devices, nothing else is required – just the art of closing your eyes and looking in. That's what meditation is: the art of looking in. And the moment thoughts disappear and the mind is utterly quiet and silent, the inner light is seen. It is a revelation. Once you have seen your light, you will be surprised: you can see it now in everybody else. Then the whole of existence is nothing but an ocean of light. It is not matter, it is pure energy.

DAY 80

For centuries, God has been thought of as light. That is because of our fear of darkness. It is not that God is only light: God is as much darkness as he is light. God has to be both; otherwise darkness would not exist at all. God has to be the lowest and the highest, matter and mind. God has to be the whole, and the whole contains the polar opposite. God cannot be only light. It is because of our fear of darkness that we have never thought of God as dark, it has nothing to do with God.

And to approach God through fear is not right. God should be approached fearlessly, in deep love but not out of fear. If you look with fear, you will project your fear. You will see things which are not there and you will not see things which are there. When you are not afraid, you look with absolute clarity. Fear is like smoke surrounding you, like clouds. And God can be seen only with clarity, absolute clarity, unconditional clarity, clarity and nothing else. Then God is both – he is as much light as dark. Then he is summer and winter, life and death. Then the duality disappears and a tremendous oneness arises in your vision. That oneness brings bliss. That oneness brings freedom.

We are bound by the dual and we can be freed only by

the one. As Plotinus says: "The search for God is a flight of the alone to the alone." Start looking at darkness as divine. Start looking at everything as divine because all is divine whether we know it or not, whether we recognize it or not. Our recognition is irrelevant – existence is divine. If we recognize it, we rejoice; if we don't recognize it, we suffer unnecessarily.

DAY 81

Man appears very finite, very small, just like a dewdrop. But he contains all the oceans, he contains all the skies. If you look from the outside, he is very small, tiny; just dust, nothing much – dust unto dust. But if you look from the inside, from his center, he is the whole universe.

That's the difference between science and religion: science looks at man from the outside and finds nothing spiritual, nothing divine, just physiology, chemistry, biology – another kind of animal. Hence scientists go on studying animals to understand man; animals are simpler, easily manipulated. So scientists go on researching with rats and whatever they conclude, they go on insisting that the same is the case with humanity. It is a little more complex of course, but basically it is the same. Science has reduced man to a rat. And man can only be understood now by studying rats or dogs: Pavlov used to study dogs to understand man and Skinner studies rats.

Man has to be understood only by understanding buddhas, christs, krishnas. Always remember that this is one of the fundamentals: you cannot understand the higher by understanding the lower, but you can understand the lower by understanding the higher. The higher contains the lower but the lower does not contain the higher. The only way to understand man is not from the outside, not through observation, but through meditation. One has to enter one's interiority, one's own subjectivity.

Standing there, one comes to know the greatest wonder and awe – that man is nothing but godliness.

DAY 82

Science goes on telling people: "You are nothing but animals. Human beings are only a species of animal." And for three hundred years they have been propagating the idea. It has penetrated very deeply into our blood and bones and marrow. We are not animals. In fact, animals themselves are not animals. We are divine, so are the animals. Religion is rooted in this vision of man being divine, of the universe being divine.

Science reduces everything to the lowest common denominator. If you bring a lotus flower to the scientist, he will say that it is nothing but mud because it grows in mud, it comes out of mud. If you bring mud to a mystic he will say, "Don't be worried – there are thousands of lotuses hidden in it, because lotuses grow out of mud." The world needs again a religious vision. My effort here is to give you the perspective that you are not mud, that you are lotuses. Even mud is not mud because it contains lotuses, because it can be transformed into lotuses; it is just a raw form of lotus.

Religion looks from the highest point and makes the highest point the decisive factor. Science looks at the lowest and makes that the decisive factor. From this moment, this has to be your vision: you are divine, so is the whole universe. With that vision it is easy to move upward, because if there is no upward, no possibility of anything higher, then one forgets all about transforming oneself. If there is a possibility, one starts groping for it. The possibility is there. The buddhas are enough proof of it, enough evidence for it.

DAY 83

Everyone is God. Nobody can be anything else because only God exists: God is synonymous with existence. To *be* means to be a God. But we don't remember it, we are absolutely oblivious to it. So the question is not how to *achieve* godhood, the question is how to remember it. It is a forgotten language.

My effort here is to help you to remember something that is already there. Nothing has to be achieved. You have only to discover yourself, to discover who you are, and you will know that you are God.

And the moment you know you are God, the whole of existence becomes divine, then everybody is God. And when the whole of existence looks divine to you, it is a tremendous joy. You are surrounded by godliness. Naturally, great rejoicing arises in your heart.

DAY 84

Man is a bridge between the animal world and the world of the divine. Man is just in between, he is a passage; hence man is not really a being. A dog has a certain being, a lion has a certain being, a rosebush has a certain being, a rock has a certain being. Man has none.

Man is a becoming, not a being. Man becomes a being only when he has transcended humanity, when he has become a buddha, a christ. Then he attains to being, but then he is no longer man. He has passed over the bridge.

Pass over the bridge; remember, don't build your house on the bridge. It is something to be passed over, something to be transcended. And that is the beauty of man. No dog can be anything other than a dog; no rock can be anything other than a rock. They have a fixed being; there is no possibility of growth. Only man grows. Only man has the possibility of adventure, of journeying into the unknown. The greatest beauty of man, the greatest grandeur, is that he can surpass himself.

DAY 85

Meditation leads you toward the oceanic – from smallness to vastness, from the bounded bodymind structure to the unbounded consciousness, from the finite to the infinite, from time to eternity, from birth and death to eternal life.

The only requirement is to drop the notion of the ego, which is not difficult for the intelligent person to do. It is difficult only for the stupid – but for them everything is difficult. The more intelligent someone is, the more easily he can drop the idea because he can see that it is an absolutely wrong notion. We cannot be separate – we cannot exist even for a single moment in separation. If the breath does not go in, we are gone. We are continuously exchanging.

Breathing means the bridge between us and the whole. The breath is something like roots into the whole: when you pull a tree out of the earth, it starts dying. It loses its roots; they were its nourishment. Stop breathing and one dies. Breathing is a subtle way of our being rooted in the whole. The very word *breath* means life, because without the breath there is no life.

DAY 86

Meditation is the art of landing at your very center. We live on the circumference – how can we jump from the circumference to the center? It is a whole art. I call it an art rather than science because science is more mathematical and art is more artistic, more poetic. In science there are no exceptions, it follows universal laws. In art there are exceptions; in fact, every individual reaches his center in a slightly different way from anybody else because each individual has something unique in him. That is the divinity and the great grace of the universe – it only makes unique individuals. Meditation is the bridge between the circumference and the center, between the outer and the inner, between mind and no-mind, between matter and consciousness.

DAY 87

Meditation is the greatest miracle there is. It is the greatest gift given by the awakened ones to humanity. Science has given many things, but nothing compared to meditation. And one cannot conceive that science will ever be able to give anything comparable to meditation. Up to now, meditation has been the greatest gift ever to humanity, and it is going to remain the greatest gift forever. That can be safely predicted for the simple reason that science goes on studying the objective world; meditation gives you mastery of your subjective existence, your inner world – and the inner is always higher than the outer.

DAY 88

Each moment, die to the past and remain fresh, and your life will be a great adventure. And it is only for the adventurous people to know what truth is. The non-adventurous live in comfortable lies.

Unless you are a rebel you will not attain to fragrance. It is only through rebelling against all the rotten traditions that one becomes fragrant. Tradition stinks and if you remain part of it, you continually stink.

The past is dead, it is a corpse, and to live clinging to the past is disgusting. But that's what millions of people are doing. We have to get rid of the past. You *are* only when you are free of the past; for the first time you are, for the first time you are an authentic individual. And that authenticity brings fragrance. Your heart opens up into a beautiful flower, you become a lotus.

DAY 89

Man can live in two ways. He can live a life which is enclosed from all sides, encapsulated. There are reasons why millions of people choose this kind of life – it is safe, secure, cozy, but they are missing something far more valuable because they will miss adventure and they will miss the exploration of the truth and they will miss godliness and they will miss love, they will miss light. In fact they will miss all, and what they will get is just a comfortable death. Their life is the life of the grave.

Of course, in a grave there is no danger, you cannot die again. It is the safest place, but even though it is safe you have lost life. Friedrich Nietzsche used to keep a sentence written in gold on his table. It consisted of only two words: *Live dangerously*. Somebody asked him, "Why do you keep it there?" He said, "Because the mind always wants to slip into comfort, into the familiar, even though the familiar may be miserable. The mind always likes that which it knows well, that with which it is acquainted. It may not be a joy but still, you are on familiar ground. And bliss happens only when you move into the unfamiliar, when you go into the uncharted sea."

Godliness is possible only when one learns to live the second kind of life. The first is encapsulated. That is the choice for millions. That's why they are just walking graves – alive only in the animal sense of being alive, in fact vegetating. They don't have souls. Gurdjieff used to say that very few people have souls, and he was right because a soul needs a certain opportunity to grow, it needs challenges, it needs a kind of vulnerability, all the windows and doors open to the wind, to the sun, to the rain and to all unknown forces. When one starts living dangerously one lives for the first time. And to live dangerously is to live a divine life. Jesus lived dangerously, Buddha lived dangerously, Socrates lived dangerously, al-Hillaj Mansoor lived dangerously. But these were the people who reached the highest peak of being individuals. They came to know the Everest of consciousness.

DAY 90

This is a way of looking at things in such a way that slowly, slowly God starts emerging from everywhere. Although he has no form, he starts expressing himself in all forms possible. You start feeling him in all forms.

In one sense, no wave is the ocean; in another sense, every wave is the ocean. In one sense, no form is God; in another sense, every form is divine.

The mind cannot know because the mind can only catch hold of forms. To know the formless you will have to go beyond the mind, you will have to drop the mind at least for a few moments every day, so that you can be bathed with godliness. And those few moments are the real moments. They are the only moments that you have lived; all other moments will go down the drain. They will not be saved – only those moments that you have lived with God, with the presence of godliness, are saved.

DAY 91

Flow with the river, go with the river, abandon yourself totally to the river. It is already going to the ocean and it will take you there too: you need not even swim. And that's what I am trying to create here: a great river of dancers, singers, lovers, people who are capable of laughter, rejoicing, celebration – a river that is constantly moving toward the ocean. The ocean represents existence and unless we find it we cannot be content because of limitations, boundaries; all boundaries are bondages. The moment the river falls into the ocean it becomes infinite, it becomes eternal.

DAY 92

Life means always remaining flowing, moving. Go on reaching for the farthest star.

Enjoy the very journey and don't be too worried about the goals. Goals are only excuses so that one can go on and on in the journey. In fact, there are no goals in life. Life is a pilgrimage, a pilgrimage to nothing, a pilgrimage to nowhere – just a pure pilgrimage. To understand this brings great freedom, great unburdening. All anxieties, all anguishes drop; all worries disappear, evaporate, because when there is no goal you cannot fail. Failure is our idea because we believe in a goal.

For example, I can never fail because I have no goal. I can never feel frustrated because I never expect anything. If something happens, good; if nothing happens, far out! Either way it is always good. And that is my fundamental teaching.

DAY 93

I don't want you to belong to a church, to a creed, to a nation, to a race; those are all ugly things. One should be free of all that nonsense. One should be simply human.

There is no need to be a Christian, or Hindu or Mohammedan, and no need to be an Indian, an American or a German. One should be free of all those bondages. They are prisons which keep your spirit encaged. Break out!

And it is all up to you. If you cooperate with all these things you are cooperating with your slavery. Stop cooperating. Nobody else is keeping you in bondage. It is your own unawareness. So become aware of how you cooperate with your slavery, and that very awareness is enough to get rid of all slavery. Freedom is your nature. It is not to be achieved. When all slavery disappears, one is free; when the slavery is no longer present, freedom starts welling up within your being. And out of freedom, life starts taking on tremendous beauty. Then everything is possible – love, truth, godliness.

DAY 94

We are seeds but it would be unfortunate to die as a seed. We have to become flowers and we have to release our fragrance;

only then is there contentment. A tree is fulfilled when it blooms, when the spring comes and the tree has released, poured, its heart into colors, into fragrance, into joy. When the tree is dancing in the wind, in the sun, it is fulfilled. Exactly the same is the case with man too. A buddha is a tree which has bloomed, a christ is a tree which has come to release its fragrance. We are all carrying the same kind of seeds in us. Everyone is a buddha unmanifest, a christ ready to be born at any moment. My work here is to make you aware of your great potential, of your infinite possibility, of the heights that you can reach, of the depths that you can penetrate. Your heights are higher than the Himalayas, and your depths are deeper than the Pacific. And once you know your heights and your depths, life becomes nothing but gratitude. Existence has given you so much. It has poured all its creativity into your being, it has made you so rich, so inexhaustibly rich.

DAY 95

As you live, more experiences, more memories accumulate, and it becomes a mountain – really heavy. People are crushed under it. The moment you see that it is useless you can drop it. It is not clinging to you, you are clinging to it, so you simply take your hands away.

Then the next thing that comes through watchfulness is that you become aware that the future is not yet, so why be bothered about it? When it comes we will see, we will respond.

There is no need to be worried about it – it may never come or it may come in such a way that you cannot imagine it right now. It is unpredictable. Whatever you think about, ninety-nine percent of it is never going to happen. And wasting your energy for that one percent is sheer foolishness.

Once you see it, you withdraw from the future – and the past and the future are one hundred percent of your mind, the whole content. Fifty percent belongs to the past and fifty percent to the future. In the present there is no content. If one is just here now, then consciousness is empty. You can see that whenever you look in your mind, either something from the past is moving or something from the future. As far as this very moment is concerned, consciousness is pure.

And the meditator starts settling in the present by slowly, slowly dropping the past and the future. To live here now is to live a religious life. That is pure consciousness, and out of pure consciousness whatever happens is virtue. Whatever you do is right. Whatever your response you will never repent for it, you will never feel guilty for it.

DAY 96

My effort is to help you to accept yourself as you are and to go on searching and seeking for your authentic soul. It is burdened with so many stupid ideas that you will have to unburden yourself, empty yourself. Only by emptying all the nonsense that has been given to you by others will you be able to have the first contact, the first connection with your being. It is a tremendous freedom. It is freedom from time, freedom from mind, freedom from death. Suddenly you enter the dimension of eternity; suddenly you become contemporaries of God. Less than that is not worthwhile.

DAY 97

Deep down in the heart it has to be understood that life is a gift of tremendous value: that each moment is precious, that it has not to be wasted, it is a great opportunity to grow. One should not go on collecting colored stones and seashells on the sea beach. Something more important has to be done, something more significant. One has to look inward. One should not remain concerned just about outside things because that's how people waste their lives. One should start searching within: "Who am I?"

One should go deeper and deeper into one's consciousness to feel one's center. The moment that you feel your center, all questions are answered, all puzzles disappear. There is no confusion anymore. Everything is clarity, a transparent clarity. You can see through and through. And that is the moment when one understands how much the universe has given to us, and how ungrateful we have been to the universe. Gratitude is the basic requirement for a religious life. It is out of gratitude that prayer arises, it is out of gratitude that love arises, it is out of gratitude that grace arises. But one can feel gratitude only if one feels the value, the immense value of life, the inestimable value of existence.

DAY 98

Existence is unbounded, infinite, vast. Existence is oceanic and we are like dewdrops. We have to learn the art of disappearing into the ocean. It needs guts, because to disappear into the ocean means to die as a dewdrop. But unless one dies as a dewdrop one cannot be born as the ocean. When the seed dies as a seed, a great tree is born. The seed disappears: only through its disappearance does the tree appear.

DAY 99

Once you are awakened, you start living life in a totally different way. Although your life remains the same you are no longer the same.

Your approach is different, your very style is different. You live more consciously. You don't go on groping in darkness. You live through the heart and not through the head. Your life becomes love, compassion. It becomes a song, a dance, a celebration. And of course whosoever comes in contact with you will be infected by it. It is contagious. It is like fire, wildfire; it goes on spreading.

DAY 100

For God there is no darkness. For light there is no darkness. Darkness exists only when light is absent; hence they never meet. Light does not know at all that darkness exists. How can light know? When light is present, darkness is not. Darkness is only an absence. God knows no darkness. And we know only darkness – that's how we have been unbridged from God.

We too have to reach a point where darkness disappears and only light remains. The day darkness disappears for you is of great celebration, is a day of great blessing. It is possible only when you realize that you are light.

DAY 101

Become blissful, become luminous. The flame is already there. You have not to do anything, you just have to discover it. It is within you, so you have not to go anywhere. Just be in silence, be still, looking in, searching. You will have to pass through a big crowd of thoughts and desires, but it is not as big as it appears from the outside. Yes, you have to push and pull a little bit and you have to force yourself inward a little bit. But it is a beautiful game, it is fun; to meditate is fun. And once you have been able to pass through the crowd into the open space of your inner being, you will see the flame. That's your inner being.

That flame is part of the great flame of existence, part of the universal fire.

DAY 102

The moment you speak a truth, it becomes a lie; utter it and you have already made it false. It remains true only when it lives in deep silence within you.

My effort here is to help you to read your inner being, because only there will you find the virgin truth, unpolluted, uncorrupted by words, language, scholars, priests, interpreters, commentators. It is only within your own being that you will find the still, small voice of God. Just one condition has to be fulfilled: you have to become silent, noiseless, so that you can hear it; so that you can read it.

DAY 103

In your true reality you are a god. You may have fallen asleep and you may be dreaming that you are a beggar, that you are a man or a woman, that you are white or black, that you are this or that, that you are poor or rich – but all those are just dreams. When the mind stops dreaming only one thing remains, and that is: "I am God."

To die without knowing this is to have lived in a futile way. One is fulfilled only when one knows, "I am God." And it is not a question of believing. The priests have been saying for centuries that the Kingdom of God is within you – but that doesn't help. You need to experience it on your own. Being Christian does not help, only being a christ can help. Buddhism is not going to give you the inner kingdom; it can be attained only when you become a buddha.

My effort here is not to create Christians and Buddhists and followers, but to create buddhas, awakened people, who are not following anybody but are simply living their true nature with authenticity, with responsibility, with joy.

Belief is easy; you can start believing that you are a god. That will simply be megalomania, it will simply be madness.

It is a question of experiencing.

When you believe that you are a god, when you believe "I am God," the "I" is very important and God is just a shadow. When you experience "I am God," the "I" is just a word, a utilitarian word; only God is real. "I" has to be used just for the purpose of communication, otherwise there is no I. That's the difference between the madman and the mystic. The madman can declare "I am God," but he is simply declaring "I am." His declaration of "I am God" is the ultimate ego. The mystic also declares "I am God," but he says "I am not: hence I am God."

So I am not saying to believe it. I am saying that you have to experience it. Don't leave this life without experiencing it. This is an opportunity to experience your reality.

DAY 104

Unless one realizes one's godhood nothing is achieved, life has been a failure. And one *can* realize it, it is every man's birthright; but one has to claim it, one has to work for it, one has to be very creative about it. That's what sannyas is all about: becoming alert about the great opportunity and using every possibility to grow: to grow beyond humanity, to surpass humanity, to become divine – because that is our reality.

DAY 105

Man has many layers of identification, and we have to drop all the layers, slowly, slowly, slowly. Finally nothing is left – and that nothing is you. Only nothing can be vast. "Something" is bound to be finite. Only nothing is infinite: hence God is ultimate nothingness. God is not a being but the ultimate nonbeing. He is not somebody, he is absolute nobody-ness. He is only a presence, infinite, unbounded. And so are we. We are not different from God. We are part of that infinity.

DAY 106

All that is valuable has harmony in it, as its very core. Without harmony there is no God. The harmony in existence proves that something keeps it together; something invisible. Without harmony there is no love. But it is an invisible thread, nobody can see it.

Everybody can feel it. Love makes one aware of the fact that all that is seen may not be all, there may be more than you can see.

DAY 107

Love is nothing but the disappearance of the dewdrop into the ocean. It is losing one's ego, it is total surrender to existence. It is meeting with the whole, it is dropping your boundaries and your identity. It is abandoning yourself. The moment you abandon yourself, you immediately become oceanic, vast. We are clinging to our identity. We protect it, we fight for it, we are even ready to die for it. And this is just stupidity because the ego is the most false thing in existence. It is just hot air, it has no real existence. It is like darkness.

You can see darkness, every day you see it, but it has no existence as such. It is simply the absence of light – nothing in itself, just an absence of light. Bring the light in and you don't find any darkness. You never even see it going out of the door; put the light off and it is suddenly there. It does not come in – you can keep the doors and windows closed... It comes from nowhere because it is nonexistential, It is just an absence. It does not come and go. Light comes and goes because light is.

The same is true about your ego. The ego is the absence of love. The moment you bring the light of love in, the ego disappears. You need not do anything else: just become more loving, unconditionally loving.

DAY 108

Love is not addressed to anybody in particular: just be loving – that has to be your quality. It has nothing to do with a relationship.

Love has to be like a fragrance. Whether anybody comes to know it or not does not matter to the flower. Even in the farthest Himalayas, where nobody comes and goes, thousands of flowers bloom and spread their fragrance. In the Himalayas there is a whole valley of very strange flowers. People have only seen the valley from the peaks, nobody has been able to reach it because to go down into the valley is dangerous. People know about those flowers, but nobody has smelled their perfume. And they have very psychedelic colors. Those flowers are far away, but they are not worried at all about that; they are perfectly happy. Love has to be your quality.

Become loving, and one day it happens that you are simply love: not even loving but love. That is the day of great revelation. In that very moment the dewdrop disappears into the ocean and becomes the ocean.

DAY 109

This is the whole secret on the path of love: unmotivated love transforms your whole being into love energy. And to become love energy is to become divine. Nothing more is needed. That is more than one can ask for, it is more than one can dream of. It brings absolute fulfillment, it brings flowering. You bloom.

Flowers of consciousness start opening within you.

DAY 110

Meditation only takes you up to the door. But that is the greatest journey – from the head to the heart, from logic to love, from knowing to feeling. Hence the poet is closer than the scientist, the dancer is closer than the politician, the lover is closer than the businessman. But it is only through meditation that the poet will become aware of that one step; otherwise he can stand at the door of the temple, keeping the door behind him.

That's how the poet *is* standing: standing at the door of the temple but looking out. The mystic is also standing at the same door, but looking in. They are standing on the same spot; the thing that makes the difference is meditation. Meditation gives you a one-hundred-and-eighty-degree turn; you don't look outside, you look in. The poet looks outside, he is exactly on the same spot.

It is as if you are going up a staircase and somebody else is coming down. You meet on a step, you say hello to each other. You are on exactly the same step but one is going down, the other is going up.

The directions of the poet and mystic are different. They are located in the same space, on the same step; the poet and the mystic are exactly on the same step, standing at the same door. But the poet is looking outside and the mystic is looking inside – and that makes the difference, the greatest difference.

The moment the mystic looks in, he rushes; then he cannot stop, nothing can stop him. The urge to rush in is irresistible. Meditation makes you capable of the ultimate step. So focus your whole effort, your whole being on only one thing, keep one word constantly in remembrance – meditation. Put your total energy into it so that it can become a reality for you.

DAY 111

To enter meditation, one of the most essential qualities is patience. One cannot be in a hurry. The more in a hurry one is, the longer it takes. If one is capable of waiting forever – lovingly, trustingly – it can happen even in a single moment. Instantly it can happen, immediately it can happen: it all depends on how patient one is.

But remember, while doing meditation never bother about the result. It will come in its own time. Trust! Enjoy meditation for its own sake, don't be greedy about it, don't project any ambition. If one can do meditation not as a means but as an end unto itself, then the miracle can happen immediately, it can change your total being.

The transformation is easy. One has to learn the art of being patient – which humanity has completely forgotten.

Everybody is in such a hurry, everybody wants things to happen quickly. Nobody is ready to wait. That's why there are so many charlatans in the world of religion. You ask for instant coffee so there are peddlers who sell instant coffee, and they exploit you. My approach is of patience, infinite patience – and then the miracle is that it can happen even like instant coffee. But the requirement has to be fulfilled. It is a paradox, but anything concerned with the truth is always paradoxical; it has to be paradoxical because truth needs to be inclusive of its opposite.

DAY 112

One has to be very playful about meditation, one has to learn to enjoy it as fun. One has not to be serious about it – be serious and you miss. One has to go into it very joyfully.

And one has to keep aware that meditation is falling into deeper and deeper rest. It is not concentration, just the contrary: it is relaxation. When you are utterly relaxed, for the first time you start feeling your reality, you come face-to-face with your being. When you are engaged in activity you are so occupied that you cannot see yourself. Activity creates much smoke around you, it raises much dust around you: hence all activity has to be dropped, at least for a few hours a day.

That is so only in the beginning. When you have learned the art of being at rest, then you can be both active and restful together because then you know that rest is something so inner that it cannot be disturbed by anything outer: the activity continues on the circumference and at the center you remain restful. So it is only for beginners that activity has to be dropped for a few hours. When one has learned the art, then there is no question: for twenty-four hours a day, one can be meditative and one can continue all the activities of ordinary life.

DAY 113

Meditation does two things to you: one, it makes you aware of the beauty that exists all around, it makes you sensitive to it; and the second thing, it makes you beautiful, it gives you a certain grace. Your eyes become full of beauty because the whole of existence is beautiful; we just have to drink out of it, we just have to allow the beauty to enter us. Through our eyes, through our ears, through all our senses, the beauty has to be allowed to enter us. It gives tremendous nourishment to the soul.

Ordinarily a person is not aware of the beauty that surrounds existence. He is more aware of all that is ugly because the mind always goes on finding the negative. It counts the thorns, it misses the roses. It counts the wounds, it misses the blessings. That's the way of the mind. Mind is basically negative, its whole approach is negative. It thinks only of dark things. From the past it goes on collecting dark things and about the future it goes on projecting dark things. It lives surrounded by a dark world of its own creation. And of course then life seems to be a great hell.

The moment you move into meditation, the moment you become a little more silent, a little more calm and quiet, more relaxed, more rested in your being, you suddenly become aware of the beauty of the trees, of the beauty of the clouds, the beauty of people, of everything that is there.

Everything is beautiful because it is full of godliness: even rocks are overflowing with godliness. Nothing is empty of godliness. And once you start experiencing all these beautiful dimensions, the ultimate result is that nourished by your beautiful experience – by music, by poetry, by dance, by celebration, by love – you become beautiful. A natural outcome is that a grace arises in your being and it starts radiating.

DAY 114

Roses are beautiful, lotuses are beautiful, but they are not flowers of beauty. They are beautiful flowers, of course, but not flowers of beauty. Flowers of beauty happen in your innermost core. They happen through inner growth, when you transform your potential into actuality. When you really become a being, when there is no more to life, when you have experienced life in its totality, then something flowers in you. That flowering brings you for the first time a gift from existence.

There are many gifts from existence – birth is a gift, life is a gift, love is a gift – but the ultimate gift is when your consciousness becomes a lotus. When a flower of beauty blooms in you, in Japan they call it satori, in India we call it *samadhi*. It can be translated as ultimate ecstasy.

DAY 115

Being with a master means entering a sunlit world. As the sun rises, the lotus petals start opening, naturally – they are not to be forced – and then great fragrance is released. That fragrance is bliss, peace, celebration. One has come to fulfillment, one has come to be utterly contented because one has given whatever was one's destiny, and has poured it into existence. Whatever one was capable of contributing, creating, one has done it. That is the ultimate act of creativity, and naturally after that ultimate act one feels utterly satisfied, contented.

DAY 116

Love yourself because it is only through love that you will become harmonious, that you will become one. Don't condemn yourself. You have been given a beautiful body; you have been given a beautiful mechanism called the mind. If you use it rightly it is of tremendous importance; if it becomes the master then it is dangerous. If you remain the master then there is no problem, it is a beautiful servant. And you have been given a soul – a piece of existence. One cannot ask for more.

DAY 117

Light is possible, but only through love. Without love, only darkness is possible. In the inner world, love and light are synonymous; they don't mean different things. Hence one who wants to be full of light, one who wants to be enlightened, has to be unconditionally loving.

Love without any demands. Demands make it ugly, demands destroy it. If you have some conditions attached to your love, it is no longer love, it becomes lust. And it becomes a political game, a power trip.

Let your love remain pure and let your love remain unconfined; don't create boundaries to it. Let it remain unaddressed, so that slowly, slowly it is not a question of whom to love, what to love; the only question is how to be loving. The object of love is irrelevant. Love people, love animals, love the trees, love the stars, love yourself. Unless you love each and everything, it cannot become your very breath.

And just as the body needs breath – it is its life – the soul needs love. Love is the nourishment for your soul. The more you love, the more soul you have. When your love is infinite, your soul also has infinity. When your love knows no bounds, your being also knows no bounds. That's what is really meant by god-realization: it is love-realization and nothing else.

DAY 118

Love is the surest way to real victory, but it is a very strange way, very paradoxical, because love begins in surrender and ends in victory. That's its paradox: love does not want to be victorious, but it becomes victorious. Love wants to surrender, but surrender brings victory.

And the people who try to be victorious remain failures. They may become victorious in the eyes of the world, but that is not true victory because death will take it away. True victory is that which even death cannot destroy. Think of yourself as victorious only when you have gained something of immortality. Love gives you the first glimpse of immortality, love opens the first window beyond death. One who knows love is bound to know existence sooner or later, one just has to go on deepening one's love. Be in love with love itself, then victory is going to be yours.

DAY 119

Be blissful within and loving without. One can be blissful and miserly – then bliss starts dying. It has to be shared to keep it alive and flowing, to keep it fresh and young. The old tradition of the so-called religious people has been very miserly: there was no place for love in it. Of course they were all searching for bliss and they could find little bits of blissfulness here and there, but they were very greedy and miserly. And in their greed and miserliness whatever they found was killed, destroyed, poisoned; hence they remained sad. All the saints look sad, they have long faces – with no laughter, with no love, with no sharing.

This is something very fundamental, that bliss grows as you share it, otherwise it dies. Even if by chance you discover a source of it, soon it will be exhausted. If you want it to be inexhaustible, then share, share as much as possible. And never think whether the other person is worthy or not. Those are the considerations of a greedy person, a miserly person.

A person who wants to share never thinks whether the other is worthy or not. Who cares? The whole point is to share. If he is ready to share, that's enough. Be thankful that he allows you to share your joy.

The sharing of bliss is love, and it is through love that bliss grows. The more you love, the more blissful you become: the more blissful you become, the more you love. They feed each other, they help each other. And between the two you become an integrated being.

DAY 120

The mind is a wall, meditation is a bridge. The mind disconnects, meditation reconnects.

And once you are one with the whole, it means you are one with the trees and the mountains and the rivers and the stars and the sun and the moon. Then this infinity is yours and all its joys are yours. Life starts having freedom for the first time because all limitations disappear – and that is the ultimate desire of the human heart.

We are continuously searching for the union; knowingly or unknowingly we want to merge with the whole because only with the whole does life come to its ultimate peak, does ecstasy attain its Everest.

DAY 121

Unless existence dances in you, there is no possibility of any dance. Unless existence rejoices in you, there is no possibility of rejoicing.

Remove yourself so that you don't come in between you and existence. Put the ego, the very idea of "I" aside and be utterly empty, receptive. And the moment your emptiness is total, the whole starts showering millions of joys and millions of flowers upon you. The splendor is infinite.

DAY 122

All that needs to be done is to empty oneself of oneself. And when one is empty, something mysterious, unexplainable, starts happening. Something of the beyond starts descending in you, an unknown force starts singing through you, dancing through you. That unknown force is God. God is not a person; it is only a name for all that is mysterious, for all that is beyond comprehension, for all that intellect is incapable of understanding. And to be consecrated to the miraculous, to the mysterious, is the only way to live a beautiful, graceful life.

DAY 123

All that is great is always a gift of existence. It is never our achievement; in fact it happens only when we are utterly absent. Love happens when you are absent, truth happens when you are absent, bliss happens when you are absent. When you are too full of yourself, nothing happens. Then gifts go on coming but you are not ready to receive them – the ego is very nonreceptive. We can receive existence's gifts only when we are utterly empty; the emptier you are the better.

The whole process of sannyas is nothing but emptying you of yourself. Then gifts go on coming. So much happens, and without any effort, that it seems unbelievable, incredible. One becomes aware for the first time how generous existence is. Existence is not miserly. It gives, and it gives much. It is willing to give everything, but we are not ready to receive. We don't have any space to receive its gifts. So start emptying yourself and you will be moving on the right way.

DAY 124

The god of meditation is the only true god. All other gods are inventions – inventions of crafty priests, inventions of greedy minds, inventions out of fear. The only true god, which is not an invention, is experienced through meditation because meditation requires you first to drop all thoughts, including thoughts about any god.

When all thoughts and desires have been dropped, then whatever you have come to know is not part of your mind because you have put the mind aside from the very beginning. Now there is nobody to invent anything. Now you will know that which is.

DAY 125

Slowly, slowly as consciousness becomes bigger and unconsciousness shrinks, you become blissful, more and more blissful. You start opening like a flower. We are like closed buds; as bliss comes you become a flower. In the East, we say that one becomes a lotus, a one-thousand-petalled lotus. Everybody is carrying the seed, the bud, but great effort is needed to be conscious. Unconsciousness has been our habit for so many lives that it has almost become our nature.

So from this moment, try to be more and more conscious in everything that you do, in everything that you think, in everything that you feel. These are the three dimensions. In all these three dimensions you have to become more watchful, more alert, more of a witness. Between these three arises the fourth, the witness – and that is your true nature.

Once you have learned how to create the witness, you know the secret art, you know the alchemy of transforming the dark continent in your being into light.

DAY 126

When you do something creative, a great contentment arises. When you finish a painting, a silence falls over you. You feel fulfilled, meaningful, significant; you have done something. You have participated in God's work. He is a creator and you have been a creator in your own way, a small way of course, but you have participated with God, you walked with God – maybe only a few steps, but you walked with God.

But the ultimate act of creativity is the flowering of your consciousness. After that you never leave God for a single moment. Then the whole pilgrimage is with him, within him. Naturally it is tremendously fulfilling. There can be no other fulfillment higher than that, greater than that. It is the very peak.

DAY 127

People go on doing a thousand other things, rather than coming back home. If they are miserable, they go on throwing responsibility on others. The wife is creating trouble and the husband thinks that's why he is miserable… Or the society or the state… There are a thousand and one excuses. One can always find them, they are always available. If you can't find them you can invent them. But no excuse is going to help, it simply prolongs your misery. There is no excuse for your misery except the truth – and the truth is that you are very far away from your being. So whenever you are miserable, go into meditation. Become silent, watch your misery; become a witness to it, don't become identified with it, and you will be surprised that the more you watch, the less it is. And when you are perfectly watchful it simply disappears, as if it has never been there. Not even a trace is left behind. Suddenly you will find that the same energy that was becoming your misery has become a showering of bliss. You have come home.

DAY 128

Life is something tremendously beautiful but we are unaware of it, we are blind to it. It is glory, but we are not sensitive enough to receive it.

Life is perfect but our sensitivity is almost nil; hence the whole problem is how to create more sensitivity, how to become more alive, how to be more open, vulnerable, so that we can feel the life that surrounds us. The moment we are in step with life, life is God, and there is no other God. Life knows no death, no birth. It is eternal, and we are part of that eternity. But we have gathered much dust around our mirrorlike being so that it reflects nothing. Our mind is like a layer of dust on our consciousness; hence nothing is reflected and we cannot see that which is. We only see the dust; we only see our thoughts, our desires, our memories, our dreams – and they are not the reality. Unless all this dust is cleaned away we will not be able to reflect that which is.

DAY 129

We are all strangers on this earth. Our real home is on the other shore. We are here only to be ready to grow, to experience, to mature, so that we can be accepted on the other shore. We come into this life just as children are sent to school. It is a learning place, it is not our home. Learn as much as you can, experience as deeply as possible. Let your life be multidimensional, but remember one thing, that this is not our home. So don't get attached, don't become possessive, don't start clinging; otherwise who will go to the other shore?

When the evening comes the child returns to his home. For the whole day he is in school and in the evening he comes back. The school is a necessity; without it he cannot grow. With all life's pleasures and pains, with all its foolishnesses and wisdoms, with all the joys and miseries we slowly, slowly learn balancing, centering. Passing through many, many agonies and ecstasies, something inside us matures, integrates. And when we are ready, the boat arrives from the other shore to take us back home, but only when we are ready. Otherwise we are sent again and again, until we learn the lesson.

DAY 130

I have heard a story of a great musician. He was singing a song, and the people who were listening to him were great lovers of music. He finished one song and the whole crowd said, "Again, once more." He sang it again, very happy that he had been received so well. When he finished it, the whole crowd shouted even more loudly, "Again, once morel!" He sang it again. When he finished for the third time the crowd shouted even louder.

Then he said, "But I can sing other songs too." Then someone in the crowd said, "Until you sing it right, we are going to say, 'Again, again, again.'" That's what happens in life: we are sent again, again and again. You can die, but you will be sent back until you have learned the lesson. And the lesson can be learned.

DAY 131

There are only two types of people in the world, those who complain and those who praise. The complainers remain miserable because their hearts never open up, never become a flower. Their very approach is negative. They only look at the darker side of things, they never look at the brighter side. They count thorns, they never praise the roses. To praise God means to praise existence; there is no other God. This whole existence – the stars, the trees, the people, the animals, the birds, the mountains, the oceans – this totality is what God is. God is not a person, just a name for the whole.

When you start praising the beauty of the flowers, and the silence of darkness, and the joy of the river rushing toward the ocean, something starts opening up within you. You also start growing, you are no longer closed. The praise becomes a bridge between you and existence. You become more and more sensitive, more and more poetic, more and more aesthetic. Your sensibility makes you aware of the immense beauty that surrounds us, and of the great mystery which is unfathomable, which has no beginning and no end. The feeling that we are a part of this great mystery creates great rejoicing. Praise is prayer, and bliss is the fragrance of prayer.

DAY 132

Without contributing to life, nobody can ever feel blissful. So many people search for bliss but they fail for the simple reason that they are uncreative. They don't create anything.

There is one joy, and only one joy in the world, and that is of creating something, whatever that is: a poem, a song, a little music… Whatever it is. But unless you create something you will not feel fulfilled. Only by creating something do you participate in God's being. God is the creator of the whole, and when you create a small thing, in a small way you become part of God. That's the only way to bridge the gap between you and God. No prayer is going to help; no ritual is of any significance. They are just deceptive strategies invented by clever and cunning priests.

The real prayer is to be creative. But how can you create if you don't know what your potential is, if you don't know in what direction you have to move so that you can become creative and can attain fulfillment?

The work of meditation is simply to make you aware of your own potential. It simply throws light inside you; it focuses light on your inner being so that you can read the message.

DAY 133

Man is carrying within himself a tremendous capacity for music. When I say "man" I mean every person. And when I say "music" I don't mean ordinary music. Not everybody can be a musician in the ordinary sense. Only a few have that talent; it is something inborn, innate.

What I mean by music is totally different. I mean the inner experience of harmony. It is far more musical than any music that can be created. It is uncreated music. No instruments are needed, no training or expertise is needed. All that is required of you is to listen to its deep silence. It is already there. It is your very life. The Zen people call it the sound of one hand clapping.

In ordinary music there are always two things needed for sound to be created. If you are playing a guitar, you have to use your hands on the strings. Only through the tension created by your fingers will the strings create music. But the inner music is something which is already there from the very beginning. It is just like your heartbeat; a little deeper than that, a little more mysterious than the heartbeat. It is the beat of your true heart.

DAY 134

There have been two rivers of consciousness. One is of the philosophers – Aristotle is the father of that in the West, the originator. The other is of the mystics. That is a totally different kind of river. It has nothing to do with philosophizing; it is rooted in existential experience. And it has almost always happened that whenever there was a great mystic, his followers always became divided between these currents.

The real ones, those who have understood the master, those who have really loved the master, became mystics. And those who have understood only the words of the master have become very knowledgeable, they became the philosophers.

Socrates was a mystic. Plato was his disciple but he lost track, he became a philosopher. Aristotle was Plato's disciple. When Buddha died, thirty-six systems of philosophy were born among his followers – thirty-six! Almost every possibility was exhausted by those thirty-six systems. In fact there cannot be more than thirty-six systems; that is all the possible combinations, the whole world of philosophy explored.

And the real people... Mahakashyapa, one of Buddha's most authentic disciples, remained silent, he didn't say anything. He started a totally different tradition, the tradition of the mystics. He transmitted his experience not through words, not through scriptures, but through a totally different kind of communion: the communion of the master and the disciple.

It is through Mahakashyapa that the tradition of Zen was born. He was the first, and very great mystics followed. But it is a totally different world: there is no argument about God, no argument about truth, no argument at all. Mere argumentation is not the way, but meditation; not mind, but meditation.

These people became more and more silent. And as you become silent, your inner source of blissfulness starts to explode. It is the words and theories and the philosophies which function like rocks and don't allow your springs of bliss to flow. So, from this very moment remember: my way is the way of the mystic, not of the philosopher. I believe in bliss, not in theories about bliss. And I want you to taste it, not just to think about it.

DAY 135

Life should be looked at not as prose but poetry. That's the religious approach, the approach of the mystic. He looks, not with questions in his eyes, he looks with wonder, he looks with awe. He does not think about existence, he feels it. He opens his heart; rather than using his head he throws the doors and windows of his heart open, he allows the sun and the wind and the

rain to come in. That's what I mean by poetry. The mystic is a
poet in the ultimate sense.

DAY 136

The real mystics have remained utterly silent about God.
Whenever Buddha was asked, he smiled but never answered. He
would not say yes, he would not say no, he would simply smile.
It would be a very knowing smile, a very inviting smile, very
seductive – but he would just smile. He would ask you to be with
him, to sit in silence with him, to share in his meditations, and
maybe someday you would find the answer. But he did not give
the answer himself. To me, he seems to be one of the most honest
people to ever walk on the earth because nothing can be said
about God, only silence: the true God is known only in silence.

So drop all ideas of God and become more and more silent.
One day it is bound to happen: when the silence is total, he
comes so silently, so invisibly, that you are in for a great surprise.
You don't hear his footsteps. One moment he was not there, the
next moment he is there and you are overflowing with him. You
are no longer the same person, and neither is the world the same.

DAY 137

Man is powerful when he is with existence. Whenever he
is not with existence, he is absolutely powerless. Plugged into
existence you have infinite power; unplugged you are just
empty. And unfortunately millions of people are living their
lives unplugged; hence so much misery, such feelings of impotence, such feelings of emptiness, such feelings of futility.

Everybody once in a while finds life utterly absurd. There
seems to be no sense in it. One goes on living because one is
afraid to commit suicide; one is afraid of death – one is at least
acquainted with this empty life. One never knows what is going

to happen in death and after death, so it is better to go on drag-ging yourself for the time being, and hope for the best. People are unplugged, that's the whole problem. Religion simply means the art of becoming plugged into existence again. Then you are so full of power that it starts overflowing from you. You can share it and it is not exhausted. In fact, the more you give it to others, the more you have it.

DAY 138

We live in desire. Desire means discontent. Desire means that whatever is, is not right, not enough: more is needed. And desire is never fulfilled. It is unfulfillable by its very nature.

You can have as much as you desire, but the moment you have it, desire goes on jumping ahead of you – it starts asking for more. Its greed knows no limits, it is unlimited. It is like the horizon: it looks so close – you can reach it within an hour if you run. But you can never reach it. The distance between you and the horizon will remain the same, will be constantly the same, because there is no horizon; it is an illusion. The earth is not meeting with the sky anywhere, it only appears to be. Such is the case with desire. It only *appears* that if I could reach that point, if I could attain this or that, there would be contentment. I would be happy, I would be fulfilled. But it never happens.

One has to understand desire and its futility. In that very understanding, desire disappears and one is left at home in deep peace. When there is no desire, there is no disturbance. Desire is the only disturbance.

DAY 139

Our desires are dreams, all our thoughts are dreams. And we go on continuously living in dreams because we are asleep. Dreams can exist only if we are asleep, and dreams disappear the moment we awake. Going beyond dreams means awaking.

It is time – you have slept enough, for many, many lives. Don't miss this opportunity to wake up because the opportunity is rare, and to miss it is very easy. So put your whole energy into waking up. In the beginning, it seems almost impossible – how to do it? But if one goes on trying… In sleep one tosses and turns, but if one goes on tossing and turning, it is bound to disrupt the sleep. And just a moment's glimpse of being awake is enough to trigger a new process in your being. Then more and more moments of awakening happen.

The day one becomes fully awakened, twenty-four hours a day, even while one is asleep one remains alert, aware – when the body sleeps the soul never sleeps – when one is capable of being awake twenty-four hours a day even when the body is resting, then one should feel contented. One has arrived. Before that, make every possible effort that you can. Don't leave any stone unturned.

DAY 140

We are asleep, not in the ordinary sense, but in a metaphysical sense. We don't know who we are, how can we be called awake? We don't know from where we are coming, how can we be called awake? We don't know where we are going, how can we be called awake? We don't know anything that is essential.

We know much that is rubbish: we know everything about the moon and the sun and the earth and we know history and geography, but we know nothing about ourselves. We know nothing about the knower – and that should be the primary concern of any real education. Sannyas is the beginning of a real education. Fundamentally you have to become aware of yourself, of who you are. And only you can do that.

DAY 141

To be a man is a great gift, but very few people realize it. You could have been anything in this vast universe – a rock, a cabbage, a potato, anything! And there is no court of appeal! Whatever one is, one is; nothing can be done about it. What can the poor potato do about it? But very few people realize that they are human beings and have tremendous potential to grow.

The beauty and the grandeur of being human is that it is only through being human that one can reach God. It is a first basic requirement. No other animal has any approach toward God, only man – and not even all men. Only people who are really alert and aware create a bridge between themselves and God. Without that bridge, life is meaningless and a great opportunity can be lost very easily.

DAY 142

There are many wrong ways toward God, but only one right way. The wrong ways are: one can move toward God through fear. One will only think that one is moving, one will never move. That's why it is wrong. How can you go toward God if you are moving out of fear? The natural tendency when you are afraid is to escape. You can go farther away from God, but not closer to him. And all the religions have been teaching people to be afraid of God. Religious people are defined as God-fearing. Now, that is ridiculous – a religious person never fears God, he loves him. Fear is not a bridge. If you fear God, deep down you will hate him; deep down he is your enemy, he can't be your friend. And how can you surrender out of fear? The surrender will be superficial. You will wait to take revenge.

It is because of these religions that the modern mind has taken revenge. It is because of the accumulated fear of centuries that Friedrich Nietzsche has to declare: "God is dead and now man is free." This is the whole sentence. People quote only half of it – that God is dead. The other half is as important, even more important than the first: "God is dead and now man is free." Free from what? – free from fear. There is nothing to fear if God is dead. And the next sentence Nietzsche says is: "Now you can do whatever you want to do." There is nobody to hinder you; you are no longer in a prison.

Nietzsche is just the opposite of all the priests who have been creating fear in people's minds. This is the outcome: Nietzsche is the by-product. Our century is atheistic for the simple reason that we have become tired of remaining afraid.

Man can also move toward God through greed. That is the wrong way again, because greed means you want to exploit. Greed means you have certain desires to be fulfilled through God, God is not your goal. You want money, you want power, you want paradise, you want all the pleasures of paradise. And because that can be attained only through God, out of compulsion you surrender to him. But God is the means, not the end, and to reduce God to a means is ugly, it is disgusting. God is the ultimate end: there is nothing beyond it.

These are the wrong ways. They appear to be ways toward God, but they are not ways, they are walls. The only right way is love. Love more, love deeply, love for love's sake, and you will be surprised that slowly, slowly something new starts happening around you: the presence of godliness is felt.

DAY 143

A heart full of love, loyalty, trust is exactly the definition of a religious consciousness. These qualities are needed. Without these qualities one can never become aware of godliness, of love, of beauty, of the tremendous splendor of existence.

Existence is known through the heart, not through the head, and the heart approaches existence in deep love, trust. There is no other way to commune with the whole.

These qualities slowly, slowly transform you. They transform you from doubting confusion into absolute certainty of knowing. They take you out of the chaos of the head into the harmony of the heart. Remember them.

DAY 144

Prayer does not mean saying something to God, asking for something; prayer means listening to God. If you have to say something, it can only be a thank-you. A simple yes is enough.

But organized religions all over the world have been teaching people unnecessary prayers. And people are repeating those prayers, parrotlike. They have lost all meaning, they have become pure ritual, they are just formal. You have to learn the true prayer. It consists of silence, it consists of deep listening. God wants to convey something to you. He is searching for you, but he never finds you because you are always so busy. Be silent, more and more unoccupied, more and more available, and soon you will start hearing the still, small voice within.

God does not speak from the outside, he speaks from your innermost core, he is already there. And to be connected with your innermost core is true prayer. The moment you are connected, it is so blissful, so ecstatic that you can only bow down in deep gratitude.

DAY 145

Worshippers are many, the world is full of them. Churches, mosques, temples, synagogues are all full of worshippers, but I don't call them worshippers. Their worship is only a ritual. They are simply following a tradition. They are worshipping symbols. Their hearts are not full of love, they don't really have a thirst for God; they are simply performing a social duty. Maybe they have become addicted to it; if they don't do it they feel something is missing. It is like smoking or drinking: one becomes addicted.

The ritual becomes part of your mechanical life. If you don't do it, it haunts you the whole day. So people do their prayers, they worship, they go to the temples, but it is all superficial. It does not transform them. If the worship is real, it is bound to create a new being out of you. It is going to be a rebirth.

I am not interested in rituals. I don't teach that you should say a particular prayer, that parrotlike you should repeat certain formulas in Arabic, in Hebrew, in Sanskrit – in some dead language, long-forgotten. I don't teach such gibberish. I simply teach you to love the beauty of existence that surrounds you. This is true worship because God is manifest; in thousands of ways he is available – in the trees, in the flowers, in the birds, in the mountains, in the sun, in the moon, in people, in animals. Feel him. Rather than believing, feel the beauty of existence, feel the splendor of the universe, the splendor of a night full of stars. If that cannot create awe in you, then nothing can create awe in you.

DAY 146

Live life as a song. Make ordinary life as joyful as possible; make something extraordinary out of it. Don't condemn the ordinary – that is the way of the foolish person. Transform the ordinary – that is the way of the wise. The mundane is not against the sacred, the mundane is only a stepping-stone toward the sacred.

Religions have condemned life so much; hence they have been destructive toward all joy, singing, dancing, celebrating. They praise the other world and they condemn this world. To me, this and that are one. There are not two worlds, there is only one, and if you condemn this world, you cannot praise the other. If you want to praise the other, you have to praise this. And once you learn how to live on this earth beautifully, joyously, you will become aware of the presence of godliness everywhere. So live life as a song – that is my message for you.

DAY 147

Existence is absolutely impartial, but that does not mean that it is cold. It is very warm, loving, protecting, caring. But we are not open to its warmth, we are closed.

The problem is with us, not with existence. Hence the whole effort down the ages has been a single one: to help people to open up so that they can commune with the stars and the clouds and the sun and the moon – because this totality is what God is. There is no God other than this existence. And unless you are open, fearlessly open, you will never become aware of what you are missing. You are missing life, you are missing love, you are missing truth. Sannyas means a longing to commune with existence.

Gather courage and open yourself to all the beauty and the blessing and the benediction. It is all yours. It is yours just for the asking.

DAY 148

Priests down the ages have condemned man so much that everybody feels rejected, everybody feels they are just junk. Slowly, slowly the priests have destroyed all self-respect. They have created a division in every person: the condemned part and the condemner.

The condemner they call your conscience, and the condemned part they call your instincts. This division keeps you in a constant quarrel with yourself, in disharmony. You are at daggers with yourself, and that is no way to know existence.

The first lesson is to love yourself as you are, because existence loves you as you are. That does not mean that you have to remain the same forever. In fact, this is the first step of transformation: if you love yourself you will be able to grow quicker, faster.

DAY 149

Existence is always with us; the problem is from our side, we are not with it. If existence were not with us, we could not exist even for a single moment. It is our life, it breathes in us, it beats in our hearts, it is our consciousness. It is always with us, but we are not always with it.

The moment we are also with existence, a radical change happens. Then you become aware of the meaning, of the significance, of the song of life. Then you become aware of how much has been bestowed upon you, how much has been given to you. Then great gratefulness is felt, and that gratefulness is the essential core of religion, the very soul of religion. Everything else is ritual. To feel gratitude is to be religious.

DAY 150

This is the law of existence: truth cannot be conquered but can be invited. One has to be just a host for the ultimate guest. And that's what I call meditation. Meditation simply makes you empty of all rubbish. It empties you completely so you become spacious, receptive, sensitive, vulnerable, available. And all those qualities make you passionately inviting – an invitation for the unknown, an invitation for the un-nameable, an invitation for that which will make your life a fulfillment, without which life is just an exercise in utter futility. But one cannot do anything more than that: just an invitation and waiting.

DAY 151

The only thing that is essential is awareness. And people are lost in the nonessential. They have become oblivious of the essential; they are ready to sell the essential for the nonessential. That's how everybody has sold his soul for the nonessential. That's how everybody has sold his soul and become soul-less.

DAY 152

Man has to be a lamp unto himself. Drop the whole idea that you can get guidance from scriptures, that knowledge is possible by borrowing. That is one of the greatest hindrances in the spiritual search. Nothing is needed from the outside. Existence has provided you with everything that you will need on the journey. The light is there and only your own inner light can help you to distinguish the right from the wrong, can help you not to go astray, can help you to be always moving toward godliness. Those who depend on others are simply wasting their opportunity. My effort here is to guide you; not to give you directions, not to give you certain character styles, structures, patterns, but only to help you to be yourself.

DAY 153

Dreams can be realized, all dreams can be realized. The ultimate dream, of being blissful, is so close by that it is very strange how people go on missing it. It is just within reach – everybody's reach. You have just to grope for it a little bit and it is there.

But people don't grope, or if they do, they grope in wrong directions, so life remains unfulfilled. And to live a life which is unfulfilled is agony, is hell. That's what hell is. It is not a geographical place somewhere: it is a state of an unfulfilled psychology. When there is fulfillment, there is paradise.

DAY 154

We are all hung up in the head. That is our only problem. And there is only one solution: get down from the head into the heart and all problems disappear. They are created by the head. Suddenly everything is clear and so transparent that one is surprised how one was continuously inventing problems. Mysteries remain, but problems disappear. Mysteries abound, but problems evaporate. And mysteries are beautiful. They are not to be solved, they have to be lived.

DAY 155

We are making such an effort to remain miserable. People don't see it. When they do, they will laugh at the whole ridiculousness of what they have been doing to themselves.

They are doing such great work to create misery in every possible way. They don't miss a single opportunity; they jump upon anything that can make them miserable. This approach has to be changed. And life gives you both opportunities. It gives you the day, it gives you the night, it gives you the thorns and the roses – it gives you both opportunities. And it is always balanced, it is always fifty-fifty; it depends on what you choose. The miracle is that if you choose the thorns, sooner or later you will find there are no flowers because your mind will become accustomed only to thorns. You will only be able to see thorns, you will miss the flowers; you will simply not take any note of them. And the same happens to the person who chooses flowers: he starts forgetting about the thorns, he takes no note of them. His approach becomes so positive and so affirmative that his whole arithmetic is different.

DAY 156

Reach for any door to the temple of God... You can try to reach through peace, and bliss will come and love will come and compassion will come, and a tremendous understanding of other people; forgiveness will come, a great humility, humbleness, egolessness, truthfulness, sincerity, authenticity. They will all bloom. Just reach from any direction. Try to reach from love or try to reach from compassion. It does not matter; there are many doors to the temple of God. But at every door you will need the same key to unlock it – and that is meditation, that is awareness.

DAY 157

Man, when unaware of himself, is a beggar. Man aware of himself is the greatest emperor possible because the moment you become aware of yourself, the whole Kingdom of God is yours. It has already been given to you, it is just that you are asleep. It is there, but you are not looking at it. Your eyes are focused on the outside.

DAY 158

Society wants you to be dead, not alive. The whole effort is how to kill you and yet use you as an efficient mechanism. And society has succeeded: it has destroyed aliveness and replaced it with mechanical efficiency. Its whole interest is in protection, even at the cost of life. It is more interested in commodities than in human growth. Hence society goes on preaching to people to be peaceful, to be obedient, not to disturb, and it praises such peace as if it is something divine, something of ultimate value. But one can become peaceful in this way only if one is stupid – if one can't see the cost one is paying for such a dead peace, which is not worth anything at all. He is losing his freedom, his intelligence, his joy, his love, his whole quality of being adventurous.

His whole being is lost; he becomes a convenient cog in the wheel, a replaceable part. If *A* dies, he can be replaced by *B*; if *B* dies, he can be replaced by *D* or *C* because they were not individuals, they were only functionaries. All the religions have tried for this; there has been a conspiracy between the priest and the politician to destroy humanity.

A few people have rebelled against it, and it is good that a few people rebelled, but then they fell into another extreme. They dropped the whole idea of peace as useless, worthless, as a political strategy to dominate, and they were not ready to be dominated by anybody. They chose to be blissful, joyous. But a bliss without peace is feverish; it is excitement but tiring, and ultimately there is no fulfillment in it. It keeps you hot, burning hot; it gives intensity to your life. And if this is the only possibility, to choose between a cold peace and a hot bliss, then I will say choose hot bliss. At least you will be alive – feverish but alive; you will go crazy but you will be alive! You are bound to go insane sooner or later, but at least you will be alive!

If this is the only alternative, then I am all for bliss. But it is not the only alternative; it is the other extreme. My effort is to create a higher synthesis in which peace and bliss are two aspects of the same coin. Then a tremendously beautiful phenomenon happens: you have bliss but you are not hot, and you have peace but you are not cold. You are exactly in the middle, neither hot nor cold.

DAY 159

We are not aware of how precious we are. We are not aware of the inexhaustible treasure that we are carrying within us. And because we are not aware of it we go on desiring small things, quarreling about mundane things, fighting, competing for something trivial. The moment you become aware of your own inner beauty, all this struggle on the outside disappears. Life becomes calm and cool. Life attains a grace. One is no longer interested in the nonessential.

DAY 160

Awareness is what the alchemists have been searching for: the elixir, the nectar, the magical formula that can help one to become an immortal.

In fact everybody is immortal, but we are living in a mortal body and we are so close to the body that the identity arises. There is no distance to see the body as separate. We are so immersed in the body, rooted in the body, that we start feeling we are the body – and then the problem arises: we start becoming afraid of death. Then all the fears, all the nightmares, come in its wake.

Awareness creates the distance between you and your body. It makes you watchful of both your own body and mind, because body and mind are not separate. Bodymind is one identity – the mind is the inside of the body. And when you become aware of bodymind, you immediately know you are separate from both and a distance starts happening. Then you know you are immortal, you are not part of time, you are part of the eternal. You know there is no birth for you and no death either, that you have always been here and will always be here.

DAY 161

Life is full of divine glory but we are unconscious. We are so deeply asleep that we go on missing the glory of it. It is the most perfect existence possible, the most beautiful, the most magnificent. It cannot be improved upon. But we are asleep; hence we cannot have any connection to it. It is as if it is spring and the trees are flowering and the birds are singing and the wind is dancing through the trees and you are asleep.

You will not know the sunrays coming to you through the trees, and the beautiful patterns they are creating around you. You will not see the flowers, their colors. You will not see the dance of the trees and the wind. You will not even know that you are in a garden! You will have no connection with the spring. You will be enclosed within yourself. You may be having a nightmare and you may be suffering in your nightmare; you may be screaming, crying and weeping. It has no relationship with the reality surrounding you. That's exactly the situation of man.

Existence is always in spring, but one has to be awake to know it, to feel it, to live it. And once you have tasted of the joy that surrounds you, you are religious – great gratitude arises in you, and thankfulness and prayer.

DAY 162

Put all your energies into one effort: how to be more aware. And if one puts one's total energies into awareness, it is bound to happen – it is our birthright. But one should not be half-hearted. It can't happen halfheartedly, it happens only when you are a hundred percent in it, into it, when nothing is held back, when you have put all your cards on the table, the trump card included, when you are not hiding anything. When you put yourself into it totally, it happens immediately. And that happening is a great revolution. It transforms you from the lowest to the highest, from the gross to the subtle, from the visible to the invisible; it takes you from the mind to no-mind.

And to live in no-mind is to be wise. To function out of no-mind is to function out of wisdom. Then your life has beauty, grace, godliness. Then whatever you do is right. It can't be wrong; it is impossible to do wrong because you are so full of light and so full of insight, your vision is so clear and unclouded that it is impossible to do anything wrong. The right happens of its own accord. There is no need to cultivate any character; just consciousness is enough: character follows like a shadow.

DAY 163

To know oneself is to know all. And that is the only thing I emphasize: no belief, no dogma, no creed, no church, no religion. By a simple process of inner observation you come to realize yourself. And the moment you know who you are, immediately you know the essential core of all existence, of life itself, because you are part of it.

DAY 164

Life can be just a heap of flowers or it can be transformed into a garland. Yours is just a heap of flowers, it has no organic unity, it is only a crowd of many selves, of many "I's," all struggling and fighting for supremacy. Man lives in a constant inner war, and every self tries to pull you in a different direction. You are always falling to pieces. Life can be lived in a totally different way. Those flowers which are separate can be connected by a thread, by something that runs through all of them, by a sense of direction, by awareness, by being more conscious. Then life is no longer accidental, then it is no longer a crowd; you start having an integrated being.

And the more crystallized and integrated you are, the more joy is possible. How much bliss you will be able to receive depends on your integrity. The fragmentary person remains miserable, the integrated person attains bliss.

DAY 165

A humble heart is one of the greatest virtues for one who is in search of truth. Only those who are humble can know truth. The egoists are prohibited; the ego itself becomes the barrier, it cuts you off from existence. Ego means you are thinking you are separate from the whole, and you are not. We are not islands, no man is an island. We are part of an infinite continent. The ego gives us a false feeling of separation, and because of that false feeling of separation slowly, slowly we become enclosed in ourselves. We become too self-conscious, self-centered, utterly closed to the world, closed to the sun, to the moon, to the wind, to the rain. We become encapsulated; that is a kind of living death. We start carrying our graves around ourselves. It is an invisible grave, but it is a grave all the same.

DAY 166

Life in its reality is unbounded, it is infinite. It is not confined to the body, not confined to the mind either. It is not confined at all; it is oceanic. Even oceans have certain limits, but life has no limit at all, it has no beginning and no end.

But we have become too identified with the body and the mind. We have completely forgotten that this is not our reality. The body is only a caravanserai, a guest house. We have lived in many bodies.

This is not the first time that you are staying in a hotel. You have stayed in many. And even though it is a five-star hotel, it is only a hotel. You are not it; you are the traveler, the pilgrim, the life, the consciousness that goes on moving from one body to another, from one mind to another, from one form to another. The day we realize that we are formless is a great day: it is the day of revelation. After that we are never the same again.

DAY 167

Man is like a dewdrop. Existence is like the ocean, and we are trying to keep ourselves separate from it. That is the root cause of our misery. Only one thing is needed: jump into the ocean so the dewdrop disappears.

It does not really disappear, it just loses its small boundaries.

It becomes oceanic, it becomes the ocean itself. But in a sense it disappears. You cannot find it anymore. It loses its old identity, its old nameplate, and its old address. It has become part of such vastness that there is no way to find it, it cannot stand out. That is the fear. That's why we go on keeping ourselves away from the ocean.

Sannyas means an effort to gather courage to disappear into the ocean. The day you die into the ultimate is the greatest day in life because then you become the ultimate. It is not death. It is resurrection. Time dies, eternity is born. Finitude dies but infinity is born. Smallness dies but greatness is born. It is worth trying.

DAY 168

Dissolve into the divine, just as a river dissolves into the ocean. Don't think yourself separate from existence. Meet, merge, more and more. We go on insisting that we are separate. That is the only irreligious act: to emphasize separation. To emphasize unity is religion.

It has to become a conscious effort. Seeing a sunset, dissolve into it. Don't just remain an observer; let the observer and the observed become one. Slowly, slowly you will learn the knack of it. Then sitting by the side of a tree you can have a deep feeling of unity with the tree. These small experiments can lead you ultimately to feel oneness with the whole, and that experience is godliness.

DAY 169

To remember "I am God," means to remember "I am the sky." All the experiences that happen in life are like small clouds; they come and go, they are not worth paying much attention to. Take no notice. Let that be your meditation. Remember always that you are the sky, the infinite sky, no clouds can distort you.

Slowly, slowly the clouds will not come to you. They never come uninvited. You may not have invited pain, but you invite pleasure, and pain is the other side of the same phenomenon. Invite one and the other comes. They cannot be divorced, they are always together.

When you stop inviting them, these guests start disappearing.

DAY 170

Meditation is the real beginning of life. The first birth is not the beginning of life. The first birth is only the beginning of an opportunity to live. The first birth only makes you potentially alive, not actually alive. That potentiality has to be transformed into actuality, only then do you become really alive. And meditation is the art of transforming the seed into the flower. It is through meditation that one attains the second birth.

With the first birth the body is born, with the second, the soul. And only when we come to know that we are a soul is our life fulfilled; otherwise it is a sheer waste. The seed remained a seed; it never sprouted, it never became a tree, it never flowered. Nobody rested under its shade, no birds ever came to visit it, no winds danced around it. There was no dialogue with the clouds, the sun, the moon, the stars. The seed cannot communicate with existence. It is closed, encapsulated within itself.

Meditation opens you up. Meditation is nothing but opening multidimensionally to all that is: to the beauty of existence, to the music of the winds, to the freedom of the clouds, to all the mysteries that surround you, to all that is without and within.

DAY 171

People live in a very gross way, with anger, with jealousy, with possessiveness, with ego.

How can you be a poet? You can be a murderer, but you can't be a poet. Even if you write poetry, your poetry will be full of blood. One should remove all these gross elements from one's being because they are destroying so much energy, wasting so much opportunity. All those energies should be transformed into songs, into joy, into love, into peace. Then life becomes poetry. Then it is a sheer joy to be.

Just to *be* is more than one can ask for, just to breathe is enough proof that existence is, because each single breath brings so much ecstasy with it. Life becomes such a harmony and melody, such a dance that one cannot believe it is possible. One can believe it only when it happens.

DAY 172

The ego is the only problem, and then it creates a thousand and one problems. It creates greed, it creates anger, it creates lust, it creates jealousy, and so on and so forth. And people go on fighting with greed, with anger, with lust, but it is futile. Unless the root is cut, new branches will keep coming. You can go on pruning the branches and leaves, but that is not going to help. In fact by your pruning, the tree will become thicker and thicker. The foliage will become thicker and thicker. The tree will become stronger. My insistence is: don't fight with the symptoms, go to the very root of the matter, and that is simply one – it is the ego.

Cut it from there and all other problems disappear as if they had never existed. If you can learn just to be without the ego, to be as if one is not, to be a nobody, nothingness, then the ultimate is achieved. There is no goal higher than that. And it can easily be done because the ego is a false phenomenon; hence it can be dropped. It is not a real thing. It is imaginary, it is a shadow. If you go on believing in it, it is. If you look deeply into it, it is not found at all.

Meditation simply means looking deeply inside for the ego,

searching every nook and corner of your being. It is not found anywhere. The moment it is not found anywhere, it is finished and you are born anew.

DAY 173

Not to be is the only way of really being. So I cannot agree with Shakespeare that to be or not to be is the question. It is not the question at all, because not to be is the only way to be!

The moment you disappear as an ego you become vast; you start experiencing oceanic, unbounded ecstasies. But we are too attached to the mind, which is a very tiny thing, a very small biocomputer. And we are attached to the body, too identified with it. It is just a small hut. Live in it, keep it clean, keep it beautiful. Use your biocomputer, take care of it as one should take care of every mechanism − and it is a very subtle and delicate mechanism − but don't become identified with these things. It is just like a driver becoming identified with his car. Of course he is in the car, inside the car, but he is not the car. That's actually the case with us: we have become identified with the mechanism in which we are living. And this identification creates the idea of ego: "I am the body, I am the mind. I am Christian, I am Hindu, I am white, I am black, I am this, I am that…"

All these things are nothing but identification. Meditation means becoming unidentified, just remembering: I am only consciousness, watchfulness, awareness, a witness. In that witnessing the ego dissolves; and the dissolution of the ego is the greatest revolution. You are suddenly transported from a small, ugly world into the vast and the beautiful, from time to eternity, from death to immortality.

DAY 174

It is one of the greatest mysteries of life that we are born with perfect bliss in our being and we remain beggars because we never look into our own selves. We take it for granted, as if we already know all that is within. That is a very idiotic idea, but it prevails all over the world. We are ready to go to the moon to seek and search for bliss; but we are not ready to go inside ourselves for the simple reason that, without ever going in, we already think: "What is there inside?" We somehow go on carrying this notion that we know ourselves. We don't know ourselves at all.

Socrates is right when he says: "Know thyself." In those two words, all the wisdom of all the sages is condensed because in knowing thyself all is known and all is fulfilled and all is achieved.

DAY 175

Heaven is not somewhere else; you have to create it just as you create hell. It is a psychological state. And once you know that you are the creator, there is great freedom. If the other is responsible, you are not free: you are always in bondage because the other can always create misery for you or can create happiness for you. In both ways you are dependent, and nobody likes dependence.

DAY 176

Man lives unconsciously; he goes on doing many things because others are doing them. He goes on following and imitating. He is not exactly aware of why he is doing these things, he is not even aware of who he is. What else can you expect when a man is not aware of who he is, from where he is coming, to where he is going and why?

These are the basic questions which can be solved only through meditation. No philosophy can help you to solve them. It will supply many, many answers but all the answers will be hypothetical and if you ponder over them you can always find many flaws, many faults. Meditation is existential, not philosophical. It helps you to become so aware that you encounter yourself.

Meditation makes you a vigilant spirit. You are full of consciousness. As unconsciousness starts receding and consciousness starts claiming more and more ground, your life becomes more and more centered, more and more fulfilled, more and more joyous, more and more significant. And when all the darkness of the unconscious has disappeared and you are full of light, just pure awareness and nothing else, all the mysteries are revealed to you.

Truth is a revelation, not a conclusion of thought – a revelation in meditation, not a conclusion through mentation.

DAY 177

Purity is when you live in a choiceless awareness: when you are neither concerned with the good nor the bad, when you don't divide at all, when you accept everything as divine, when divisions have been dropped, when you see only the one. Even in the Devil you see God; and even in darkness, light; and even in death, eternal life. When the ordinary ways of seeing things as dual are dropped, you become pure because then nothing can contaminate you. That is the ultimate state of consciousness.

We have to transcend all duality: moral–immoral, good–bad, life–death, summer–winter. All have to be transcended so that one can see the one. One can see the one in so many millions of forms; one is capable of recognizing the one wherever, in whatever form he appears.

It is possible. All that is needed is a little effort to become more awake, a little effort to be aware and choiceless; just sitting inside, watching the mind, not choosing anything.

The traffic passes by, you sit by the side unconcerned, cool. Slowly, slowly a purity starts descending on you. That purity is liberation.

DAY 178

Learn awareness. Become more and more alert about everything that you are doing and about everything that goes on in your mind and moves in your heart. Be aware of these three layers: the body, the mind, the heart – actions, thoughts, feelings. Be aware on all these planes and slowly, slowly that awareness starts settling and the fourth is born in you. When the fourth is born, godliness has penetrated you. The fourth is your soul, your innermost core. And the revelation of it reveals to you that you are unborn and that you are not going to die, that you are part of eternity.

The very feel of eternity is ecstatic. Your whole perspective changes. It is the same world, but it is no longer the same because you are no longer the same. Jesus says again and again, "Unless you are like small children you will not enter my Kingdom of God." But that does not mean that children are in the Kingdom of God, otherwise they would not lose it. Who can lose the world of God, the Kingdom of God for mundane things? They are not in it, they are unaware of it; hence the emphasis: those who are *like* small children. Remember the word *like*: he is not saying those who *are* small children, he is saying *like* small children. One thing is certain, they are not children; they are like small children. That's the definition of a sage: he attains a second childhood.

DAY 179

The true mystic is not an ascetic, is not self-torturing. He loves life, he enjoys life, because life is nothing but existence manifest. A true mystic is full of songs. Each of his words is a song. Rightly understood, each of his movements is a dance; rightly understood, each of his gestures is a celebration.

This happens only because of the ultimate state of consciousness. When you have touched the highest peak, when there is no more beyond, when you have gone beyond the beyond... When everything is left behind, the body far, far away, down in the valley, the mind also somewhere on the way, and you are just pure consciousness, just a pure mirror reflecting nothing, no content, just pure consciousness, no object, just pure subjectivity – that is called *samadhi*. And then thousands of songs will start arising in your being, thousands of flowers will bloom. Unless that happens, no man is fulfilled, no man can ever be content, no man should ever be content before this happens.

One should carry a divine discontent within one's heart. One should go on carrying the divine discontent for this ultimate goal. One should become an intense longing to achieve *samadhi*, to achieve superconsciousness. It is possible, because it has happened to other human beings: to Jesus, to Buddha, to Zarathustra, to Lao Tzu. It can happen to you, it can happen to everybody. It is everybody's birthright; we just have to claim it.

DAY 180

Be of the heart. Slip out of the head and move toward the heart. Think less, feel more, and finally, even feel less: be more. These are the three stages: thinking, feeling, being.

We are at the point of thinking, but we have to be at the point of being. Then there is wisdom, wisdom that liberates: liberates one from the body, liberates one from the world, liberates one from all limitations, liberates one from personality and makes one capable of merging with the universal. Just as a river disappears into the ocean, the man of the heart disappears into existence.

DAY 181

People live as biological units and die as biological units. Very few people have attained to their spiritual selves – and those that do are the only real people. Everybody has the potential but people never work on it, so it remains just a potential and it is lost. It *can* become actual. So make it a point that from now onward your whole life will become a concentrated effort to become more and more conscious. And as glimpses of consciousness start arising in you, you will be surprised: bliss follows each moment of consciousness. As consciousness deepens, bliss deepens. Bliss is the consequence, the by-product of being conscious.

DAY 182

I don't teach purity, I don't teach morality – that is all non-sense. I teach only meditation, so you can get rid of the mind. The mind belongs to society and meditation belongs to you. With meditation you are absolutely free, and suddenly you start discovering your intrinsic treasures. And then begins a great pilgrimage of joy, beauty, songs, celebration. It is an unending process. It gives you the vision of eternity. It gives you the certainty that you are immortal.

DAY 183

Society needs every child to go through school, college, university – almost one-third of life is wasted to force the energy toward an unnatural center, the head, and to create barriers so that the energy does not go through the heart. The natural process is that the energy comes from the being to the heart and from the heart to the head. This is the natural process, and if the energy comes through the heart then the heart remains the master and the head becomes the servant. The whole trick of so-called education is to avoid the heart completely and create a direct track between the being and the head, and to ignore the heart.

It has been done: the heart is left by the side and the energy starts moving from the being to the head. Then the head becomes the master. And the head as a servant is beautiful, but as a master it is very ugly. My effort here is to undo what society has done to you. But it is not as difficult as society's work; it does not take twenty-five years. It can happen even in a single moment. It needs only a clear-cut understanding.

The moment you understand what society has done to you, you can immediately open your heart, and the energy starts flowing through it because that is the natural way. It is how it should be.

DAY 184

Nothing is wrong with you except that you have believed in all kinds of fools — you have not listened to your own heart. You have listened to all kinds of people who know nothing. Drop all that borrowed knowledge. Forget all the stupid stories of original sin and forget all about being a sinner. Everybody is part of existence, an intrinsic part. Everybody is divine. Yes, a few divine people are fast asleep — that is their choice. And a few people are awake — that is their choice. Nothing is wrong even in being asleep, you just have to suffer a few nightmares. But there is nothing much to worry about because those nightmares are just imaginary. Sooner or later you will wake up. And if you are enjoying it, enjoy! It is nobody else's business to interfere.

So I don't interfere in your sleep. I go on doing my thing and I allow you to sleep. I cannot stop myself from doing my thing, so I go on speaking and you go on sleeping! I hope someday you will listen. Something may go into your sleep; something may hit you, someday, in some moment, and you may wake up.

I would love you to wake up, but if you decide not to, you are not to be condemned and thrown into hell. You are suffering enough just by being asleep, there is no need to make you suffer more in hell. This is the only difference between buddhas and ordinary people; otherwise they are all alike. Alike in the sense they all have the same potential to become awakened, not alike in the sense of being similar – they are unique.

DAY 185

Man ordinarily gathers dust around his being and loses the brightness which is his birthright. Everybody is born bright and everybody becomes mediocre. By the time one dies, one is almost stupid. This is a strange phenomenon. And people call it evolution – it is involution.

Children are brighter, more alive, clearer about everything, without any confusion. As they start growing, they start gathering confusion from everywhere. We wait until they become twenty-one years of age then we give them the right to vote because by that time everybody has lost their brightness, everybody is dull, stupid. Then you are called adult. You are really adulterated, completely adulterated. But people say, "Now you have become an adult, you have come of age." Certainly politicians are afraid to give voting rights to children because they will see through and through. Voting rights can be given to you only when you have lost all the capacity to see, when you are utterly blind.

My effort here is to help you to drop your rust, your dust; to cleanse your mirror, so you can again see your original face.

DAY 186

The whole structure of society is against the heart; it trains the head, it disciplines the head, it educates the head. It neglects and ignores the heart because the heart is a dangerous phenomenon. The head is a machine.

Machines are never rebellious, they cannot be. They simply follow orders. Machines are good in that way – they are obedient, hence the state, the church, the parents, everybody is interested in the head. It is convenient for all. The heart creates inconvenience for the status quo, for the established order, for the vested interest. The head functions through logic. It can be convinced for certain purposes; it can be argued with, persuaded, conditioned. It can be made Christian, Hindu, Mohammedan, it can be made communist, fascist, socialist. Anything can be done with the head. And whatever you feed the head, it goes on repeating. It can't bring a single new thing, it is never original.

The heart lives through love, and love cannot be conditioned. It is essentially rebellion: one never knows where love will lead you. It is unpredictable, it is spontaneous; it never repeats the old, it always responds to the present moment. The heart lives in the present, the head lives in the past; hence the head is always traditional, conventional, and the heart is always revolutionary, rebellious. But you can be victorious only through the heart, through love, not through logic.

DAY 187

The whole history of humanity begins with the Garden of Eden: man has been expelled from the garden and since then he has been wandering in a desert. Somehow he remembers the glory of that garden – those days, those timeless days before he was expelled.

The biblical story is not just a story, it contains a great truth. Every man feels that something is missing, that he is not where he should be. He may not be very clear about what is missing, but a vague feeling that something is wrong is felt by everyone: "I am in the wrong place, in the wrong situation. I am not supposed to be like this. Something has gone wrong." Man was expelled from God's garden. The reason for his expulsion was that he tried to be knowledgeable, he ate fruit from the tree of knowledge. The moment one starts being knowledgeable, one loses contact with one's heart – and the heart is the real garden. We are carrying it within ourselves. We are not really expelled. We have simply forgotten it, we have ignored it. We have become hung up in the head, we have become too attached to knowledge. Instead of growing in being, flowering in being, we are simply collecting information, sheer futile information.

It may help you to be an egoist but it can't help you to be blissful. Bliss has nothing to do with the head, it is not a function of the head. Bliss is the flowering of the heart. The heart is the Garden of Eden, the paradise, the *firdaus*. And my whole effort here is to help you to in some way enter the garden again. Even if you have to be smuggled in, it's okay, I don't bother about that – even through the backdoor… Once you have reached the garden, once you have tasted it again, you will be transformed.

DAY 188

Man can have knowledge, but not wisdom. Knowledge is easy, you just need a little effort by the mind, a little exertion. You can go on feeding your memory system. It is a computer; you can accumulate whole libraries. But wisdom is not something that you can accumulate because it does not happen through the mind at all. It happens through the heart, it happens through love, not through logic.

When the heart is open with love, with trust, when the heart is surrendered to the whole, then a new kind of insight arises in you: a clarity, a tremendously deep understanding of what life is about, of who you are, of why this whole existence exists in the first place. All the secrets are revealed, but through love not through logic, through the heart not through the head. Existence has a direct connection with the heart, no connection with the head at all.

So if one wants to approach existence, the way is through the heart. Once you have known wisdom through the heart, then you can use your mind as a good servant, then you can use even the knowledge accumulated by the mind in the service of wisdom – but not before you have known through the heart.

DAY 189

Humanity now knows more than it has ever known before: knowledge goes on accumulating. In fact, you know more than Jesus. If you meet Jesus you can teach him many things. He will not know a thousand and one things. I don't think he will be able to pass the matriculation examination – impossible! But that does not mean that he is not a knower. He knows, but in a totally different way. His experience has transformed his being.

He is not as informed as you are but he is transformed, and that is the real thing. Information means nothing. A computer can have more information than you have, but the computer can never become a christ or a buddha. Or do you think a computer can become enlightened some day? That is impossible.

A computer can know everything possible, but it will remain a computer and it will repeat only that which is fed into it. It cannot be blissful either – what bliss can a machine have? It cannot be loving either – how can a machine be loving? It may say, "I love you, I love you very much: I am ready to die for you." It may say beautiful things, but they will simply be words. It can be taught to hug you and kiss you, but there will be no love at all. And you will know that this is just foolish – a machine kissing you and hugging you. You will look all around, embarrassed!

A machine can be taught these things and the machine can do these things very efficiently. But millions of people are doing exactly that: functioning like machines, computers. They repeat clichés – Christian, Hindu, Mohammedan – beautiful words, but all dead.

With me, it is not a question of becoming more informed. I am not a teacher, I am not here to teach you anything. On the contrary, I am here to help you unlearn – not to learn but to unlearn, so that you can be unburdened and you can start seeing on your own.

The moment you start seeing on your own, your life takes a quantum leap into a new dimension: the dimension of eternity, the dimension of godliness, the dimension of bliss, truth, freedom.

DAY 190

Knowledge is a dead thing, knowing is alive and flowing. In fact some day in the future, we will have to evolve a totally new language because all our old languages are out of date. They were evolved by different people, for different uses, in different situations. All those situations have disappeared, but the language is a hangover.

Now we know both religiously and scientifically that in existence nothing is static. Everything is always in movement. Eddington is reported to have said, "The word *rest* is absolute nonsense because I have never come across anything like it in existence. Nothing is ever in a state of rest. Everything is changing, moving, it is a dynamic existence."

So instead of saying *knowledge* I say *knowing*, instead of saying *love* I would prefer *loving*. But we have become so accustomed to nouns that we even call a river, a river; it is just *rivering*. It is never the same even for two consecutive moments. We call trees, trees; they are all *treeing*, growing each moment: some old leaves falling, some new leaves growing. Except for change, nothing is permanent in existence.

DAY 191

From this moment, think of awareness as a question of life and death. In fact it *is* a question of life and death. Without awareness you are simply dying every day; with awareness you start living for the first time and then life goes on growing bigger and bigger, vaster and vaster.

One day it is so abundant that not only are *you* alive, whoso-ever comes close to you also becomes alive. You start imparting some magic to others too, you start overflowing with life, love, light. And that is the state of a buddha, of a christ, of a wise man, of a wise woman.

DAY 192

Mind is incapable of knowing the truth. It can gather all kinds of information about the truth, but to know *about* truth is not to know truth. To know *about* love is not to know love; to know love one needs to be a lover. No information can be of any help; one has to go into the experience itself. And the same is true about truth. You can know all the great philosophers of the world, you can accumulate great words, theories, hypotheses, and you can come to certain arbitrary conclusions of your own. But remember, they are arbitrary because they are not rooted in your experience. So whatever you know will hinder your search.

That is the greatest danger in knowledge: it can give you a false notion that you know. And once this wrong idea that you *know* enters you, then the inquiry stops. One has to know that one knows not. One has to put aside all information for and against, theistic, Christian, Hindu, Mohammedan, religious, philosophical. One has to put aside every kind of knowledge, even knowledge as such: then the inquiry begins. Then one becomes a true seeker of truth because then one is open. Out of that state of not-knowing, one day the great blessing happens that one comes to experience truth, to live it. One becomes it. That is the state called enlightenment, nirvana. In the West, they have called it the state of christ-consciousness; in the East, we have called it the state of buddha-consciousness, but it is the same.

DAY 193

One has to be as innocent as a child; then, and only then, do the doors open. The doors of the divine remain closed for knowledgeable people; the doors are completely closed for pundits, scholars, priests. They already know – they don't need anything more. They have repressed their ignorance by accumulating borrowed knowledge. They have lost the quality of wonder which is the most essential thing to existence.

The child has tremendous wonder. His heart is continuously feeling the mysterious, the miraculous. His eyes are full of awe – at small things: pebbles on the seashore, seashells… He goes on accumulating them as if he has found diamonds. And he is intrigued by such small things – a butterfly, just a flower, an ordinary flower, and he is enchanted, almost hypnotized.

These are the qualities which help you to open to godliness, to bliss, to truth, to the mystery of existence.

DAY 194

A disciple is one who functions through a state of not-knowing. Whatever he knows is only hypothetical and he is always ready to change it – he is not a fanatic. He loves truth so much that he cannot decide anything about truth in a hasty way. His love is so great that he is not in a hurry. He knows truth is vast: "How can I be decisive about it? At the most I can say that I feel this much: maybe, perhaps, this is right."

One of the greatest men the East has produced was Mahavira. He used to start every sentence with "Perhaps…" It was becoming almost annoying to his disciples, irritating. He would always start every statement with "Perhaps…" But I can see his point. This is the non-fanatical person. If you ask him "Is there a God?" he will not say yes or no; he will say "Perhaps – perhaps yes, perhaps no." He will not give you a conclusion. He will help you to inquire; he will push you into an inquiry.

That's the function of the master: to push you into an inquiry. He does not give you ready-made conclusions. He simply makes you aware of the tremendous questions of life, of the tremendous mysteries of existence.

DAY 195

Knowledge borrowed from others is untrue, knowledge gathered from the outside is untrue. It hides your ignorance, but it does not make you wise. It covers up your wounds, but it does not heal. In a way it is very dangerous because one tends to forget one's wounds, and the wounds go on growing inside; they can become cancerous. It is better to know them. It is better to open them to the winds, to the rains, to the sun. Hiding them is protecting them, and they are your enemies. It is better to let them be exposed – nature heals. Hence the first step of true knowledge is to know: "I know nothing." That is exposing your ignorance. And from that moment a turning happens, a great change happens: one starts looking inward.

True knowledge has to happen within you. It can't come through thoughts. It has to come through a thoughtless space within you. It cannot come through studying, it comes through meditation. It comes only when the mind becomes absolutely contentless, so utterly empty and pure, uncontaminated, unpolluted, that your own inner sources start flowing because all the hindrances have been removed.

The source from where the spring can flow is there, but there are many rocks in the way. Those rocks are thought to be knowledge; they are not knowledge, but the enemies of knowledge.

Drop all that you have learned from without, so that the within can speak to you, and then you will know the flavor of true knowledge, knowing. And true knowing liberates.

DAY 196

The body is small, the mind is small, but the being is vast — as vast as the ocean: in fact, vaster than any ocean because even the greatest ocean has its limits, and our being has no limits. It is infinite. It has three qualities and the first is truth. When you experience your being for the first time, you taste something of truth. Before that you had known only theories about truth. It was like a man who has known much about food, but has no experience of eating anything at all.

It is like a man who understands everything about water and is thirsty: he knows the formula, H_2O, but that formula is not going to quench his thirst. He understands intellectually what water is, of what it is made, but he has never seen it. He has never drunk water; he has never tasted the coolness, the contentment that comes when the thirst is quenched.

We have not known truth, we have only heard many theories about it. Those are all hypotheses. When you enter your being beyond the body, beyond the mind, the first taste is of truth, and the second taste is of consciousness. Otherwise consciousness is only a word.

People are fast asleep: they don't know what consciousness is. They are not conscious at all, they are like robots, functioning like machines. And the ultimate, the third thing, is bliss, *anand* — that is the peak.

As you go deeper into yourself, first you encounter truth, then you encounter consciousness, and at the very core of it you encounter bliss.

DAY 197

The scientists say that a single memory system, a single human mind, can contain all the libraries of the world; it has that great a capacity. But even if one contains all the libraries of the world, one will not be a buddha. One will still remain the same fool, the same donkey loaded with all the scriptures. It won't transform one's being. If one wants to transform the being, one has to go beyond the word, one has to go beyond all theories, ideologies, doctrines, scriptures.

Be finished with information; put a full stop to it because it only makes man a parrot – we call those parrots pundits. But it does not make one contented, blissful, loving, knowing. Put an end to all information. That means put an end to the mind. And putting an end to the mind is the birth of meditation. The cessation of the mind is the birth of meditation. And once meditation is born, then miracles start happening, then life starts taking such quantum leaps that it is unbelievable.

One starts becoming aware of so many mysteries that are all around, which are so abundantly here. But we are closed because of our knowledge. Our eyes are closed. We are blind because of knowledge. Knowledge is making us blind. One has to become innocent like a child; and the moment one is innocent – clean, completely clean like a mirror – then one reflects the truth. And to know the truth is to become it.

DAY 198

We are brought up by every society, civilization, religion, in such a way that we are given a false identity. We are all deceived and cheated. And the people who cheat us are very powerful; in fact, their power depends on their cheating and they have been cheating for centuries. They have accumulated great power – the politicians, the priests – and they are afraid of allowing anybody to know the truth. Their whole business depends on people who are gullible, ready to be deceived, very willing to be deceived – in fact asking to be deceived, hankering to be deceived. They create such situations that slowly, slowly the child becomes aware that if he wants to survive in the world, he has to compromise. It is not very conscious – you can't expect that much consciousness from a child; even old people are not so conscious – but a vague awareness starts growing in the child: "If I am going to be truthful, I will be in constant trouble." If he says anything true he is immediately punished.

Every child comes to a point many times almost every day when he has to decide that if he wants to survive he has to lie, he has to compromise, he has to adjust; if he says the truth, then he unnecessarily lands in trouble. And the people who surround him are powerful; they can torture him, they can make him suffer. Almost every child chooses survival because to survive is a very fundamental need of life.

By the time you are strong enough to be truthful, you have lost all sense of truth. Your lies have gone so deep in you, they have become so unconscious, they have become so much a part and parcel of your blood, bones, and marrow, that it becomes next to impossible to get rid of them. What the society has done to you has to be undone. You have to be reborn, actually reborn; you have to start learning things from *ABC*, only then will you be aware that the ego is a false entity imposed on you, that you are not a separate unit at all, that you are part of the organic whole.

DAY 199

It is a simple phenomenon – children learn from their elders; whatever the others are doing, children start doing. Our children see movies and TV and murder and suicide and robberies, and all kinds of things. They are learning. They see violence everywhere, rape, murder – and they start repeating the same pattern. Their children will learn from them, it becomes a routine phenomenon; everybody is searching outside, though the treasure is within.

Jesus said again and again, "The Kingdom of God is within," but even his very close followers never understood him. Even when the last night came and Jesus was going to be caught, they were asking about the Kingdom of God in heaven, and for his whole life the poor man was saying that the Kingdom of God is within you!

This was the last conversation with the disciples and they asked, "Just tell us one thing, master: in the Kingdom of God, you will be sitting by the right side of God, and out of us, your twelve close disciples, who will be sitting next to you?"

You see the stupidity, the politics, the question of hierarchy. And the poor man has been saying his whole life, "Blessed are those who are not hankering to be first, because they will be first."

But people go on listening to words, beautiful words; they appreciate them but they don't understand. We have missed Buddha, we have missed Jesus, we have missed all the great masters, and that's why there is this miserable humanity.

DAY 200

Everyone brings a truth in his being. The truth has not to be invented, it has only to be discovered, or rather, rediscovered. We are already in possession of it, but we have become completely oblivious of the fact. We have just fallen asleep and forgotten who we are. All that is needed is remembering.

George Gurdjieff used to teach his disciples only one method, the method of self-remembering. Buddha calls it right-mindfulness; Krishnamurti calls it awareness; Christ calls it watchfulness; Shankara calls it witnessing. But it is the same phenomenon. You have to become more alert, you have to become more conscious. Nothing is missing, it is just that you are dreaming – dreaming that you are a beggar, and you are not a beggar.

Once the dream is broken, once you wake up, suddenly you

realize what ridiculous dreams you have been in. The greatest treasure is yours. Eternal life is yours. The Kingdom of God is yours. The ultimate is yours. And we have brought it with us. We are it! So it is not a question of seeking and searching somewhere else, it is simply a question of putting your total energy into waking up.

DAY 201

Truth needs no defense. It is very simple, it is simply so. And the man who lives in truth need not bother what he has said, what he has done. He need not go on remembering all that he has said and all that he has done. The lying person has to be continuously calculating, watching. He may say something that goes against something else that he said before; he may do something that may undo something else. His life becomes more and more complicated, more and more entangled. It becomes a riddle, it becomes a problem; he becomes a problem to himself and to others. And a problematic life cannot know what bliss is.

Bliss is known only by the simple, the innocent. But the way to find it is to put the mind aside and to go into a state of no-mind. Slowly, slowly a few glimpses will arise, and then those gaps start becoming bigger and those beautiful intervals become vaster. And then sooner or later such a state arises that even if you are in the marketplace doing the ordinary things of life that are needed, your silence continues like an undercurrent; it goes on flowing. You can hear its melody, you can feel its beauty, you can taste its sweetness.

Truth brings many gifts, but you have to open the door of meditation. Nobody can give you the truth; truth is already given to you from existence itself. It is not something that has to be found anywhere else; it is already the case, it is your suchness. You just have to take a few steps inward.

DAY 202

The story in the Bible about Daniel is very beautiful. Mind you, I call it a story, not history, because to me, parables are far more significant than history. History records only facts. Parables record truths. Facts are ordinary. This is a parable; it cannot be historical.

Daniel was cast into a lion's den for refusing to deny his faith, but he emerged unharmed. Now, I don't believe that lions are so religious or so vegetarian. Even in olden days they were the same people – a little worse maybe...

But the parable that Daniel came out of the den of lions unharmed is beautiful. It says only one thing, that love for truth is greater than life itself, that one can sacrifice one's life for truth, but not vice versa. It also says that although man has evolved so much, still the basic instincts remain the same. Still people of trust are bound to suffer like Daniel, because society lives on untruths and it cannot tolerate a man of truth. Secondly, it says that the man of truth need not be afraid; he cannot be harmed by anything, not even by lions, because the man of truth knows something which is eternal in him, indestructible. Even death cannot take it away.

My own feeling is that if it is really a historical fact that Daniel was thrown into the den of lions, he must have been killed but not harmed. He must have died blissfully, joyously, ecstatically, because he was dying for truth. To live for lies is worthless; to die for truth is one of the greatest blessings in life.

DAY 203

Truth cannot be purchased. There is no way to get it from others, it is nontransferable. One has to discover it oneself. No money can purchase it, no power can purchase it, but if one enters oneself, one finds it. In fact it is already given, there is no need to purchase it.

The irony is that everybody has purchased it. Somebody has purchased it from the Christian marketplace, somebody from the Hindu marketplace, somebody from the Jewish marketplace, somebody from the Gita and somebody from the Bible and somebody from the Koran. But remember, whatever you have purchased from others is only something *about* truth – it is not truth. You have purchased only words – empty, contentless.

Truth is only truth when it is your own experience. Jesus cannot give it, Buddha cannot give it, I cannot give it to you. Nobody can give it to you for the simple reason that you already have it. All that is needed is an inner search, an inner penetration to the core of your being – and you will find it.

It is good that it is not a commodity. It is good that nobody can give it to you; otherwise it would have been worthless. People would inherit it from their parents, people would write it in their wills: "Half of my truth will go to my wife and half to my girlfriend and then it has to be divided equally among my sons…" It would be quite something.

It is not a thing – and it is good that it is not. There is one experience in life which is absolutely individual. That's why truth is even higher than love because love can be shared with the other, but truth cannot be shared even with the beloved. It is utterly individual; you know it in your absolute aloneness.

DAY 204

I don't teach you belief or disbelief; I teach you inquiry, and inquiry is always scientific. I trust in inquiry because I know that if you really inquire, you will find God; there is no need to believe. When I know that the sky is full of stars, why should I tell you to believe? I invite you to come out of your room and see for yourself – I trust my experience, hence I can trust your inquiry.

It is the priests who have not known God, who have not known the starry night outside, who have never stepped outside their minds, who are afraid of inquiry. They are afraid because they themselves are suspicious, they themselves have doubts – repressed, but lurking somewhere. Their doubts are repressed, but in moments of weakness they start surfacing. Hence they want everybody else to believe. They are afraid of questioning, they are afraid of asking anything.

Asking seems to them to be disobedience, questions seem to them to be irreligious: you should simply believe whatever they say… It is because they themselves have not experienced.

God is, truth is, Tao is – there is no need to believe at all. Just open the doors and the windows and let the wind and the rain and the sun come in, and they will give you a glimpse of the outside world, of the tremendously beautiful existence. They will become invitations from the ultimate. Then go and explore with joy, with thrill.

DAY 205

Truth is always there, we are surrounded by it, but we are so perturbed inside that we cannot reflect it. The full moon is there, the stars are there, but the lake is so disturbed, there are so many waves, that it cannot reflect the full moon. It cannot rejoice in the full moon, it cannot rejoice in the stars. It remains blind to the sky that is just there. All that is needed is that the lake should become a little silent.

My whole effort here is to help you to make a silent lake of your consciousness. And it is possible. If it can happen to me, it can happen to you. I don't claim any extraordinariness. Religions have done a great harm to humanity by claiming extraordinariness for their founders – because if Jesus is the son of God, then of course, he can be silent. But we are ordinary human beings; how can we attain to that height? That is his special privilege. All that we can do is worship him. We can be Christians, we cannot be christs. That is the conclusion of the whole of human history.

Krishna is God's incarnation, so perhaps it is possible for

him to be a no-mind. But how can we make it? We are just ordinary mortals, we are not incarnations of God. These foolish ideas that the founder is special have been promulgated by all religions, propagated by all theologies. Once you make the founder of a religion special, he becomes absolutely useless and disconnected from humanity.

I am a very ordinary person, just like you: no son of God, no incarnation of God – all that is bullshit. I know only one thing: that it has happened to me, it can happen to you. It can happen to anybody. Just a little effort is needed, nothing else; no special privilege of birth, just a little effort, a little intelligence that is provided to everybody. And the moment you attain an inner silence, a radical change happens.

DAY 206

The only thing to be remembered is that knowledge does not consist of accumulating information. It does not consist of learning from others; on the contrary it consists of a process of unlearning. One really becomes a knower when one becomes as innocent as a child again: when the mirror of consciousness is absolutely contentless, when the lake of consciousness has no waves, not even ripples. Then the whole sky, the whole of existence, is reflected in you in all its glory, in all its beauty, in all its grandeur.

And that experience is God. Be empty, be still. In fact, be not. Be just nothingness so that the whole can descend in you, so that the whole can be reflected by your consciousness. That experience is the only religious experience, the only mystical experience. It gives you certainty about God, not a belief, but absolute certainty. It gives you absolute clarity. Godliness becomes your own experience. It is not that Jesus says so or Buddha says so or I say so, but that you know it. The experience penetrates into your very guts, it becomes part of your being. Only then is the goal achieved and life fulfilled.

DAY 207

If one is ready to become a nobody, then one becomes the greatest. Be nothing, then you are all; be nobody, then you attain tremendous extraordinariness. Just be empty and you will come to know the greatest in you, the highest in you.

But remember: don't be nothing in order to become the greatest, because then you cannot be nothing. To be nothing is not to be used as a means to becoming the greatest. The greatness is a by-product; it is not the goal, not the end. It is like fragrance. The flower is the end, the flowering of your consciousness is all, and then suddenly there is fragrance. If you search for fragrance, you will miss the flower, and without the flower there is no fragrance. If you search for the flower, the fragrance comes of its own accord.

DAY 208

My definition of real achievement is that which cannot be taken away by death. Anything that can be taken away by death is not a real achievement but only a pseudo achievement, toys to play with. Become a nobody from this moment and enjoy nobodyness and the freedom that it brings. Become anonymous and see the joy! There is no worry, no anxiety. Because there is no ego, you don't feel hurt. Nothing can hurt you. Somebody can insult you and you can stand there watching and enjoying it because there is nobody inside you to feel hurt, there is nobody to be wounded. You can enjoy and laugh.

The day a man can enjoy and laugh while he is being insulted, he has already attained something, he has become part of eternity. He has entered the world of the immortals.

DAY 209

If you have eyes to see, you will be surprised: even a beggar is not just a beggar, he is also a human being. He has experienced love, he has experienced anger, he has experienced a thousand and one things that even emperors may be jealous of. His life is worth reading, worth observation, worth understanding, because his life is also a possibility for your life.

Each person is living a possibility, transforming a single possibility into actuality. And all those possibilities are yours too. You can be an Adolf Hitler and you can be a Jesus Christ – both doors are open. One has entered through one door, the other has entered from another door; both doors are open for you. Hence I have been as interested in Gautam Buddha as I have been interested in Adolf Hitler. I have been interested in Jesus but I have been interested in Judas too, because each human being is my possibility.

One has to understand this, then the whole universe becomes a university. That's exactly the meaning of *university*: it comes from the word *universe*. Then all situations become learning situations and all challenges become growth challenges. So slowly, slowly one creates oneself.

We are born only as opportunities, then everything depends on us, what we are going to become, what the end result of it all is going to be.

DAY 210

Everybody in the whole world thinks of himself as loving, yet the world is turning into a madhouse. People should be blissful – if there is so much love in the world, everybody should be flowering. Nobody seems to be flowering.

Something very basic is missing. My effort here is to help you become aware of all your pretensions. Once you are aware, they can be dropped. They can be dropped very easily – the whole thing is to become aware of them. They have gone deep; their roots have reached very deep into your bones, into your very marrow. So, one has to be very alert, very aware, to find all those roots. Once you have found all the roots of your false, pseudo love, you can uproot it. You can uproot all the weeds and you will become again a child and you will start life afresh from the very beginning of innocence. Then there will be spontaneity, naturalness.

DAY 211

Love is the most shining star in the inner sky of your being. The outer stars are nothing compared to it.

Once it happened that a Sufi mystic woman, Rabiya al-Adabiya was sitting in her room, meditating with closed eyes. A friend, another mystic, Hasan, was staying with her. He went out – it was a beautiful morning: the sunrise was so beautiful, so colorful; the birds were singing; the flowers were opening and the air was fragrant. He called out, "Rabiya, what are you doing there, sitting in your room with closed eyes? Come out – God has created a beautiful morning! Come and see his beautiful creation."

Rabiya laughed and said, "Hasan, I know that as you are saying it, it must be true. But I am seeing godliness itself inside. So rather than calling me outside, why don't you come in?" Hasan felt ashamed. He came in, fell at the feet of Rabiya and said, "Forgive me. I have never known the inner. I have wasted my whole life seeing the outer."

The outer is beautiful, but nothing compared to the inner. And in the inner world, love is the most shining star, the sun. It is the very soul of your inner world, the very source – go in and find it. And when you have found it, share it, celebrate it.

DAY 212

If you forget what it means to be light, you will forget what it means to be delight-full, because they are two aspects of the same phenomenon. To be light is a basic requirement for delight to happen.

Delight happens only in light moods. Don't take life as a problem – it is not a problem at all. It is a mystery to be lived, not to be solved – enjoyed, danced, loved, sung, but not to be solved. It is not a riddle which is a challenge to solve. It is a challenge to explore, with wonder, with awe, just like a small child.

DAY 213

Nobody is imperfect; hence nobody needs to be perfect. All that is needed is to live your life totally. Perfection is already there. We come from the perfect; hence we can't be imperfect. We are born out of the ultimate, we are waves in the ocean of God. So whatever is the quality of God is the quality of the waves.

If God is perfect, we are perfect. So the very idea of becoming perfect is absurd. There is no need to become perfect, everyone is already perfect. But we are not living that perfection in its totality, we are living at the minimum. We are not using our potential, we are using only a minor part of it – scientists say not more than seven percent. Ninety-three percent potential is simply lost. And it was already there, available for us to use. We have all the money that we need, but we are living like a beggar, for the simple reason that we have completely forgotten about the treasure. The function of meditation is to remember it, to discover it. And the only way to discover it, the only way to remember it, is to live more totally, more intensely, more passionately – so that more and more potential is transformed into the actual. When you live a hundred percent, you are really using the great opportunity that God has given you. And only at a hundred percent does transformation happen, never before.

So my effort here is to make you love life as intensely as possible, to live each moment as wholly as possible, and slowly, slowly something starts unfolding in you and you start discovering yourself. The more challenges you give yourself, the more you discover.

DAY 214

You have to live in the world, but you have to think of it only as a big drama. I am against renouncing the world. You have not to escape from the world; you have to live in it, but in a totally different way. Don't take it seriously, take it very light-heartedly, take it as a cosmic joke. It *is* a cosmic joke.

DAY 215

I am proposing a totally new approach to religion. Religion has to be life affirmative. It has to enhance your life, it has to make it more beautiful; it has to be creative, not escapist. It has not to dull your senses but to make them more sensitive.

To me there is no God other than life itself, and there is no temple other than existence itself. Then everything becomes a divine celebration. And when I say everything, I mean everything: life is celebration, death is celebration; meeting is celebration, departing is celebration; childhood is celebration, youth is celebration, old age is celebration – different kinds of celebration.

DAY 216

Love is the most healing force in the world. Nothing goes deeper than love: it heals not only the body, not only the mind, but also the soul. If one can love, then all one's wounds disappear. Then one becomes whole – and to be whole is to be holy.

Unless one is whole, one is not holy. Physical health is a superficial phenomenon; it can happen through medicine, it can happen through science. But the innermost core of one's being can be healed only through love.

Those who know the secret of love know the greatest secret of life. Then there is no misery for them, no old age, no death. Of course the body will become old and the body will die, but love reveals to you the truth that you are not the body, you are pure consciousness; you have no birth, no death. And to live in that pure consciousness is to live in tune with existence. Bliss is a by-product of living in tune with existence.

DAY 217

My emphasis is on love because if love happens, then everything else happens. There is no question about it. A loving person cannot avoid encountering godliness for long. Even if he wants to escape from it, he cannot; he will find godliness, he is bound to find it – it is inevitable.

DAY 218

One who loves, is loved by the whole existence. Existence just echoes us from all directions, from all dimensions. If we sing a beautiful song, the song comes back to us a thousandfold more beautiful, it showers back on us. Whatever we give is given back.

People are miserable for the simple reason that they are giving misery to others, they are giving pain to others. This is the whole philosophy of karma. It is a very simple fact of life.

Whatever we sow we reap. And of course, if you sow a single seed, you will reap thousands of seeds. Existence is not miserly, it gives abundantly, but it can give only when you have given already – it multiplies that which you give, so everything basically depends on you. If you want bliss, shower bliss on everyone, on everything. It you want love, love. If you want anything, wanting is not going to help – do it, materialize it, and soon you will be surprised: whatever you have given always comes back to you, multiplied a thousandfold, not less than that.

DAY 219

You get only that which you have – because that which you have becomes a magnetic force; it attracts something similar to it. It is as if a drunkard comes to a city; soon he will find other drunkards. If a gambler comes to the city, soon he will become acquainted with other gamblers. If a thief comes to a city, he will find other thieves. If a seeker of truth comes to the city, he will find other seekers.

Whatever we create within ourselves becomes a magnetic center, it creates a certain field of energy. And in that field of energy things start happening. So if one wants the blessings of existence, one should create whatever blissfulness one is capable of; one should do one's utmost and then a thousandfold bliss will be yours. The more you have, the more will be coming. Once this secret is understood, one goes on becoming richer and richer inwardly. Deeper and deeper is one's joy. And there is no end to ecstasy – one just has to begin in the right direction.

DAY 220

Meditation will teach you two things: meditation as far as your inner world is concerned, and love as far as existence is concerned. Meditation has to be your center – awareness, a silent watchfulness; and love has to be your circumference, a warmth for no reason at all – because it is so beautiful to be warm. It is so delightful to be warm.

At the center be meditative, at the circumference be loving, and you will see the whole of existence change. It is the same existence; in fact *you* are changing, but immediately, as you change, the whole of existence changes with you.

DAY 221

Man can live in two ways: either he can live partially, fragmentarily, or he can live totally. Ordinarily people live in a partial way, half-heartedly, lukewarm. They don't know what intensity is, they don't know what passionate living is. They never get involved in anything. They go only so far, never whole-heartedly to the very end. They are too clever and cunning to do that, too calculative to risk that much. But unless you risk all, you will not be able to know the beauty of life. One has to be one hundred percent involved, committed, only then does life reveal its secrets.

Be total in whatsoever you do. Each act has to become an opportunity to be total. That's my whole teaching – the long and the short of it.

DAY 222

Peace is divine, it is God's gift. And God is very fair: if you are going into meditation earnestly, sincerely, you will be rewarded. There is no question about it, it has always happened that way. But one thing has to be remembered: peace is God's gift. We cannot do anything about it directly, but we can create the right situation in which it descends from above.

It is like flowers: you cannot do anything directly about the flowers but you can prepare the ground, you can sow the seeds, you can help the plant to grow, and wait. In the right season, at the right moment, the flowers will come; your effort will be rewarded. But you cannot pull flowers out of a seed, nor can you pull flowers out of a tree; you have to allow them to happen. They come from some unknown source, some mysterious source, but they always come. One has to be patient enough. One has simply to do one's work and trust that whenever the time is ripe, the flowers will come. They have always come. They came to Jesus, to Buddha, to Mohammed; they are going to come to you too. God has no favorites, he is neither for somebody nor against somebody. God simply means the ultimate law of nature.

Just fulfill your task and nature immediately responds.

DAY 223

One should start enjoying just sitting silently for no reason at all, with no motive at all – just for the sheer joy of sitting silently, just breathing, being, listening to the birds or watching your breath. Slowly, slowly a new fragrance starts arising in your being. That fragrance is meditation, that poise, that calmness, that stillness. It comes from beyond as a gift.

And whenever someone is ready, it always happens – inevitably. Nature is never unfair to anybody. Whosoever deserves and whatever he deserves, he gets. If people are miserable they deserve it, that's what they deserve. Nobody else is at fault; nobody else is responsible – they have earned it. They may have forgotten how they have earned it, they may not be conscious how they have got into the mess, but that's what they have been doing. It is the outcome of their own work. If somebody is blissful, that simply means he deserves it. Nature always gives you that for which you have become worthy, for which you are ready and prepared, and receptive to.

DAY 224

Patience is a fundamental quality of the seeker. Impatience is a barrier in the search. You can't be in a hurry as far as God is concerned because God lives in eternity, and hurry means you are counting minutes and seconds and hours. That won't do. If you want to know godliness, if you want to know truth, you have to know the way of eternity. That's why patience is needed.

Forget all about time, don't be in a hurry, don't be impatient. Wait. Wait lovingly with great expectancy but no expectation, full of joy that the guest may be coming any moment. But don't feel frustrated if he has not come yet. Keep everything ready to receive him. Go on preparing. If he has not come, that simply means you are not yet ready. So there is nothing to feel frustrated about. Just look around, prepare and prepare and prepare. The moment your preparation is perfect, your silence is perfect, your emptiness is perfect, he comes – immediately he comes!

DAY 225

The world is a great challenge if you can learn the art of being silent among all distractions. Only then, if your silence is true, authentic, alive, can godliness come to you. Godliness is life. A dead peace is absolutely worthless. So be in the world, but don't be of the world. Live in the world, but don't let the world enter you. Move, pass through the world, but remain unaffected. It is possible. It is the greatest miracle but it is possible. And when it becomes possible, one knows for the first time what ecstasy is.

DAY 226

A real man of peace will have to go through an inner trans-formation, only then does the dream become a reality. Meditation is the alchemy of transforming your aggressive energies into peaceful energies. It transforms your violence into love. They are not different, it is the same energy.

And remember always: energy is neutral, it is neither good

nor bad. Energy used non-meditatively becomes dangerous. It is a sword in a small child's hand: either he is going to harm himself or somebody else. If no harm happens, it will be simply an accident. If harm happens, that is not an accident at all; it was bound to happen, it was inevitable.

We have energies, but we are not grown-up. Hence our energies go berserk. Meditation is the process of growing up.

DAY 227

Humanity has praised hardness greatly, particularly in man: for centuries, man has been a male chauvinist pig. He has praised all that is aggressive, cruel, violent, warlike, and he has condemned all that is feminine. It is because of this that a great problem has arisen. The problem is that everything beautiful is feminine, and if you condemn the feminine, the beautiful disappears from the world. We have struggled hard to destroy the beautiful. The ugly has dominated the beautiful; the hard has been praised against the soft.

Lao Tzu says, "Don't be hard like a rock, but soft like water." He calls his way of life "the watercourse way." And he says, "Ultimately the soft wins over the hard, the rock will disappear one day. Let the water go on falling on it and the rock will be reduced to sand." Of course, right now you cannot see it happening. It will take time, but the rock cannot destroy the water. To see this, one needs a little deeper insight – a longer vision, a bigger perspective. And we are very shortsighted. We only see so far. Because of this shortsightedness, the rock seems to be worth choosing, not water. Those who have seen reality in its true perspective of eternity say something totally different: let softness be the gift.

DAY 228

Gentleness is one of the most divine qualities because the first requirement for being gentle is to drop the ego – the ego is never gentle. The ego is always aggressive, it cannot be gentle. It is never humble, it is impossible for it to be humble. Its whole project crumbles if it becomes humble. And gentleness is the way to reach existence.

One should be more like water than like a rock. And remember always: in the long run, the water becomes victorious over the rock.

DAY 229

If your life becomes compassionate, that is the proof, a concrete proof that you have gone through an inner transformation. All tensions have disappeared and there is now absolute calm, absolute silence, absolute peace. You have arrived home. Compassion becomes the symbol, the criterion, the manifestation of what has happened at the innermost core of your being. Meditation happens inside, compassion is its outer expression, its manifestation. Nobody can see anybody else's meditativeness, but everybody can see the compassion, the love, that surrounds such a person. He becomes love, he becomes compassion.

Go deeply into meditation so compassion can be achieved. That is the ultimate truth of life.

DAY 230

Learn to be more and more silent, learn to be more and more still. Enjoy silence and stillness. Those are the basic preparations for the ultimate guest. When you are in profound silence, you are capable of becoming the host to godliness.

DAY 231

Your religion has to be not out of fear, but out of love. Don't be afraid of hell – there is no hell, there never has been. It is a fiction created by the priests to exploit humanity; they have exploited humanity for centuries. And there is no heaven either. It is the other side of hell, the other side of the fiction – it is to exploit your greed.

Greed and fear are not different phenomena but two sides of the same coin; the fearful person is always greedy, the greedy person is always fearful. In fact they are not two energies at all, but two poles of the same energy. Just like the negative and positive poles of electricity, inseparably together.

There is no heaven either. Yes, there is a certain kind of hell and heaven, but it is psychological, within you. It has nothing to do with any place, somewhere below the earth or above in the sky. It is not geographical. Drop the idea of heaven and hell – religion has nothing to do with all that nonsense. Drop the idea of God as a person. To call God "the father" is simply to provoke your fear because each child has been afraid of their father from the very beginning.

That fear remains for your whole life. Even if you go through years of primal therapy, it remains and lingers somewhere, it becomes so ingrained that it goes to your bones, to your very marrow. To call God "the father" is simply creating a childish fear in you, a childish dependence in you. There is no God as a person and there is no super-father in heaven. God simply means the whole of existence; it is another name for life. Love life, be devoted to life, live life as totally as possible. Offer yourself to life totally without holding anything back, and then great bliss arises, bliss that has a beginning but no end.

DAY 232

When you move inward, the people who have gone in cannot leave any footprints for you. It is impossible because everybody's inner territory is so different. Buddha's footprints won't help you, and if you follow Buddha's footprints literally, you will never find yourself.

Jesus' map won't help you; you cannot follow it literally. It can help you in a very indirect way; it can make you aware of certain things inside, but in a very vague sense. It can give you the confidence: "Yes, there is a world inside." There is no doubt about it because so many people cannot be lying. Buddha, Jesus, Zarathustra, Lao Tzu, Mahavira, Krishna, Mohammed – such beautiful people cannot be lying. They cannot be in a conspiracy, for what? They never existed together – they lived in different ages, in different countries – yet they all speak almost the same language.

You cannot follow Buddha's footsteps exactly because his inner territory is different. Each individual is unique, so unique that you have to discover yourself all alone; hence great courage is needed.

This is the greatest adventure in life, and one who goes on this adventure is blessed.

DAY 233

Life is music, mind is noise. And because of the noisy mind we are unable to hear the music of life. Unless we stop the mind and its noise we will never come to know the beautiful music of life.

So the whole effort here is to help you in two things. First is the negative part: how to stop the noisy mind. And second is the positive part: how to train your ears so that you can hear your own inner music. If these two things are fulfilled, nothing else remains. Life achieves its ultimate peak, its bliss and benediction.

DAY 234

Music comes very close to the experience of godliness because godliness is the ultimate music of existence. It is another name for the harmony that exists in the universe. What we call music is only a tiny drop of it. But even though it is a tiny drop, it contains the whole secret of the ocean. That's the attractiveness of music: it releases meditation in you, it releases the imprisoned splendor. For a moment all the walls of the prison disappear. For a moment you are transported into another world. For a moment you transcend time and space, you become infinite, unbounded. That is the beginning, the beginning of a journey that never ends.

Music was born in deep meditation. Music is an effort to create on the outside the same circumstance as happens within you in deep meditation. Hence a real meditator is the true musician. He may play, he may not play. He may compose, he may not compose. But he knows the secret, he has the golden key, and the true musician is bound to stumble sooner or later on the fact of meditation. He cannot avoid it for long; it is inevitable because the outer provokes the inner, it challenges the inner music that is fast asleep. And the same music is hidden in the whole of existence; hence I call music one of the most divine phenomena in existence.

DAY 235

Meditation is music, the ultimate music: music without sound, music of silence. It is far richer, far deeper than any music that we can create through sound because sound is after all, a disturbance. We can make the disturbance lovable, but still it is a disturbance.

Silence means no disturbance, nothing stirs, but there is great music, there is great harmony in that wordless, soundless state. Meditation leads into that state of silence and unless a man knows that silence, he is not aware of what he is carrying in his heart. He remains unaware of his own kingdom, of his own richness, of his own treasures. He remains a beggar, while he can be an emperor any moment – just by turning in. Silence is alchemical: once you have penetrated the barrier of sound, once you have passed the barrier of sound and reached the very core of your being, you have reached the very center of existence.

DAY 236

Follow music in the outer world and in the inner world. There is no need to go to any other temple, music is enough. Learn to listen to the music of existence: the wind passing through the pine trees, or the sound of water, or the ocean in a tremendous dance. Listen carefully, attentively, listen mindlessly; listen without thinking, so that it can penetrate to the very core of your being.

DAY 237

Life is a school. We are here to learn something, and the most important thing to learn is how to sing, how to dance, how to rejoice. All of that becomes possible through meditation. Meditation releases all those energies in you. And thousands of flowers start blooming in your being. Then paradise is no longer after death, then paradise is now and here. And when paradise is now and here, only then is it a truth.

DAY 238

The first step toward truth is cheerfulness, a deep inner dance. One has to drop all that prevents that dance, one has to drop all that prevents one's life becoming a celebration. And we are all carrying many conditionings which are against blissfulness.

In fact, religion has become almost synonymous with seriousness. Religious people look so sad, as if it is a sin to laugh. They cannot sing, they cannot dance, they cannot enjoy anything. They are against life. That is not the way to find the truth.

Love life, love the small things of life, the very small things. Eating, walking, sleeping – just the ordinary activities of life have to be transformed into delight. They have to be done with such joy that they all become a dance. Then truth is not far away, then each moment it comes closer and closer. The very moment your bliss is total, truth descends into you. And truth liberates.

DAY 239

If one can become laughter, if one can become love, then there is no need of any other prayer: one has already entered the divine.

I have never seen any sad person enter the divine. The only way toward godliness is the way of dancing. So learn to dance, sing, celebrate, rejoice; and then you will find godliness everywhere. Then each experience is divine and the ordinary starts changing into the extraordinary, the mundane disappears into the sacred. The whole of life becomes so god-full that it is not a question of God somewhere above in the sky. Wherever you are, you are surrounded by godliness. You are always walking on holy ground. Then each stone has a sermon in it and each rock is a scripture. One just needs a heart, a dancing heart, to see, to feel, to be!

DAY 240

I am in tremendous love with the world and life, and I teach my sannyasins to be great lovers of life. Dance with the wind, dance when it is raining, dance with the trees, and you will be surprised that religion is not in the scriptures, it is spread all over existence. You may have its glimpses from a rainbow, you may have its experience from the dance of a peacock or a cuckoo calling from a faraway distance, or somebody playing on a flute.

Religion is not something dead. Religion is very much alive, and you have to be alive to make contact with it. If you live in misery, you live in death. If you live in bliss, you become more and more alive. When your bliss reaches a peak, an orgasmic peak, then you contact existence. That contact gives you the proof that life is not only matter but something more. And that something more is indefinable. You can call it *xyz*, enlightenment, Tao, truth, godliness, but these are just words to indicate something which cannot be contained in any word.

DAY 241

My whole vision is that of a dancing, singing, loving, laughing humanity. I would like to fill the whole earth with laughter, with music, with poetry, with paintings, with creativity, with more sensitivity. And the more sensitive a person is, the more creative, the more religious he is: the more creative he is, the closer he is to the creator, obviously. So rejoice in life — remember, that is my message to you!

DAY 242

Wisdom is a song. It is not seriousness, it is playfulness; it is not sad, it is celebrating. And unless wisdom is a song, it is not true. Then it is just knowledge, mere knowledge. It is only pretending to be wisdom. But real wisdom that can also become a song, that ultimately becomes a song, is born only out of meditation. There is no other way.

DAY 243

Life has to be rejoiced, life has to be lived in its totality. That is not indulgence – and if it is indulgence… God has created this life and he does not seem to be an ascetic, otherwise why these flowers and rainbows and butterflies – for what? Will an ascetic God create so many flowers, so many colors? So many trees, so many stars?

Darkness would have been perfectly sacred. In fact, an ascetic God would not have created any kind of beauty; he would have made everybody so ugly and disgusting that nobody would have ever thought of love. But he makes people beautiful. He makes people lovely.

God is not an ascetic – that much is absolutely certain. God is love, a creator, a poet, a singer, a dancer.

God is not a neurotic person and he is not a perfectionist at all, otherwise he would have created the perfect world in the very beginning. There would have been no evolution at all; he would have created everybody a saint. Everybody would have been born a saint and there would have been no need of any religion, of any growth.

But God creates opportunities to grow. He is not a perfectionist: he loves growth, he loves inquiry, he loves people discovering themselves. He is tremendously interested in people growing on their own accord. He accepts that sometimes they will go astray; otherwise they cannot grow. And he accepts that they will commit mistakes; without committing mistakes, nobody can ever learn.

DAY 244

Rejoicing in life is the way to God. Dance your way to God, laugh your way to God, sing your way to God! And God must be tired of your serious saints by now; for centuries those stupid guys… Either he must have committed suicide, seeing all those saints – I cannot even keep their pictures in my room – or he must have gone mad, or he must have escaped. It is impossible to conceive of God living with all those Christian, Hindu, Jaina saints – impossible to conceive.

If you look at life, if this life is a creation of God, if this life is the expression of God, then he is a dancing God, full of flowers and fragrance, full of songs – very creative, sensitive – full of music. If this life is any proof – and except for this life there is no other proof – then God cannot be a serious person.

DAY 245

Meditation makes you aware of great music – music without and music within. It is there, but we are not alert, we are not awake; hence we go on missing it. Otherwise the whole of existence is nothing but music. That music is called God by the mystics. God is not a person, but the ultimate harmony of existence; it is an orchestra. Everything is in tune with everything else. The trees are in tune with the earth, the earth is in tune with the wind, the wind is in tune with the sky, the sky is in tune with the stars, and so on and so forth. There is no hierarchy. Even the smallest blade of grass is as significant as the biggest star. They both contribute to the orchestra of existence. They both enhance it, enrich it.

DAY 246

We have nothing to offer existence but we can sing, we can dance, we can play on a beautiful instrument. We can transform our whole life into a song, into a dance, into a festival – and that is the only true offering to existence. Plucking flowers from trees and offering them to existence is stupid because those flowers belong to the trees, not you; in fact they are already offered to existence by the tree. They were alive on the tree and you have killed them, you have destroyed their beauty; you are offering existence corpses.

You cannot offer the words of Jesus; they are his words, his songs. They are beautiful, but they are borrowed. They have not arisen in your heart, they don't have your heartbeat, they don't have your signature on them. You can offer the beautiful songs of Krishna, Buddha, but all are borrowed. My basic approach toward existence is that every person has to have his consciousness grow into a flowering tree. Each person has to come to blossoming.

And of course, man's flowers will not be like the flowers of a tree; they will not be like roses or lotuses or marigolds. Man's flowers will be of a totally different category: they will be of love, they will be of freedom, they will be of joy, they will be of a higher quality. I call them songs. When the singer loses himself in his song, in that moment he has offered the song to existence. When the dancer loses himself in the dance, the dancer has offered his dance. These are the only offerings which are accepted, these are the only prayers which are heard and fulfilled. And when you start offering your joy, your love, your songs to existence, you will be surprised that the more you offer, the more goes on showering on you; it comes back a millionfold.

DAY 247

Everything is going on in such deep accord, but man remains unaware of it. That unawareness becomes his misery and he starts suffering from his own invented nightmares. Otherwise life is a celebration; it is a constant celebration, a continuum, a never-ending festival. We just have to become a little more silent to be able to hear it. And when we are absolutely silent – not only silent, but we *are* silence – then we disappear, then we are part of this whole cosmic harmony. That is the meeting of man with existence, of the part with the whole.

We disappear in one sense, we dissolve in one sense – as an

ego, as a person – but we become the whole, so in another sense we *are*, for the first time. The dewdrop disappears but becomes the ocean. It is not a loser, it loses nothing. It loses only its small boundaries that were not worth keeping. In fact they were creating its whole trouble: the fear, the trembling, the constant fear that the sun will rise and it will disappear, it will die... Mahavira has said that man's life lived as an ego is just like a dewdrop hanging on a blade of grass, constantly afraid.

Just a small breeze and that's the end: the dewdrop falls into the earth and disappears. Or soon the morning will be there and the sun will rise and the dewdrop will evaporate. How can one live surrounded by so much death?

All our boundaries are in fact drawn by our death; we are defined by our death. The moment we lose our boundaries, we lose our death too. Then we are eternal, then we are infinite.

Remember that meditation is succeeding if you become more and more alert to the great music that is always there – it just needs a sympathetic ear. Meditation creates that ear, that heart.

DAY 248

Life starts only when you start moving in the dimension beyond death. That's what meditation is for: a strategy, a device, a ladder, to go beyond death. And just a glimpse of the beyond is enough. Then you know that only the body is going to die, not you, and that only the body is born, not you. You were here before your birth and you will be here after your death. You are part of eternity. When one experiences this, life becomes blissful, and in that blissfulness one feels blessed by existence. Then naturally, spontaneously, gratitude arises.

DAY 249

Prayer is like a flower. Bliss is like the spring when flowers open up. And when the flowers open, there is fragrance; the imprisoned fragrance is released. When prayer starts overflowing with no effort, naturally, spontaneously, when you are just thankful – for no particular reason at all, just to *be* is enough, just to exist for a single moment is enough...

To attain to that fragrance is to come to the peak of your life, to the crescendo. There is fulfillment and tremendous contentment. One has arrived home.

DAY 250

The ancient seers of the Upanishads have a beautiful prayer. It is one of the most beautiful prayers ever uttered: "*Tamaso ma jyotirgamay* – oh my lord, lead me from darkness to light. *Asato ma sadgamay* – oh my lord, lead me from untruth into truth. *Mrityorma amritam gamay* – oh my lord, lead me from death to deathlessness."

This is a beautiful prayer, the most beautiful. But five thousand years have passed and I feel that now it needs a little improvement.

I would not say "Lead me from darkness to light" because darkness does not exist. I would say "Lead me from light to more light." I would not say "Lead me from untruth to truth" because untruth does not exist; I would say "Lead me from truth to more truth." I would not say "Lead me from death to deathlessness" because death does not exist; I would say "Lead me from deathlessness to more deathlessness, from life to more abundant life, from perfection to more perfection" – if that is possible, because ordinarily we think perfection means the end, but I don't think it is so.

Perfection can become more perfect; perfection goes on becoming more and more perfect. At each stage it is perfect, but still that perfection is not closed, it is open. It can always become richer, it can always become more colorful, with new songs, with a new dance, with new celebrations. There is no end to evolution.

DAY 251

There are only two types of people in the world. The first type always asks for more and never enjoys that which is available: when that which was asked for becomes available, they will still ask for more. They are never going to enjoy. They will postpone enjoyment their whole life. Their life is nothing but a long, long postponement; it is always tomorrow. Today they have to work, today they have to earn, tomorrow they will relax and enjoy. But tomorrow never comes, it is always today. Hence they live without knowing what life is.

The second category enjoys that which is there, not bothering about more. And the miracle is that every day they have more and more to enjoy. Their capacity to enjoy increases. They are constantly practicing it, each moment they are enjoying; they become more skillful in enjoying, they become connoisseurs of joy, they become very, very sensitive about small nuances of pleasure. All their senses become alive, they become tremendously intelligent.

And out of this intelligence, awareness, and sensitivity, the next moment will be born. Of course they will be able to enjoy the next moment more than they have enjoyed this moment. Their life will be a constant process of deepening; they will be moving into depth.

DAY 252

We are born with the capacity to be perfect, we are born with all the potential to reach the highest peak. But it is a potential – it has to be made actual. And to make it actual you will need a certain methodology. It is just as gold is found in the mines and then it goes through many processes of refinement. It is just as diamonds are to be found in the mines, but then they are just stones. Only jewelers can recognize them: ordinary people will not be able to recognize that they are diamonds.

Man also is a rare diamond, but ordinarily you will find anger, greed, hatred, lust, all kinds of poisons in him – and you will not be able to see any Buddha, any Christ at all. You will not be able to see Krishna anywhere, you will not hear the flute of Krishna inside him, and you will not see the purity and the innocence of Buddha. But he contains the purity of Buddha, the innocence of Mahavira, the rebellion of Jesus, the song and the dance of Krishna, and the infinite wisdom of Lao Tzu. He contains everything that has ever happened to any human being in the world.

A certain science is needed, and that's the science of meditation. It is not a complicated science at all, very simple, but sometimes it happens that we go on missing the simplest thing in life. We miss the obvious because we are always looking far away. We are always attracted by the distant, by the far away, and the closest always remains available. But it is always available, who cares about it?

Our own being is so close, and the method of meditation is so simple – that's why millions of people miss it. Once you start going in, you will be surprised that it is such a simple phenomenon but it has tremendous beauty, the greatest joy possible, the greatest flowering possible. How had you missed it for so long? You will not be able to explain to yourself why and how you waited so long. And it can transform your whole being into gold.

DAY 253

Once you enter the world of meditation, your vision, your perspective immediately changes. You start feeling that you are not here by accident, that you are fulfilling a certain need of existence.

Existence itself is behind you, but it can be discovered only in deep silence, when your thoughts, your mind, your ego completely cease. In that clarity, when all the clouds have disappeared and the sun shines forth, in that light, life is immediately transformed. It starts having meaning, significance, and with meaning and significance come joy, bliss.

DAY 254

Just as every tree is rooted in the earth, every consciousness is rooted in godliness; godliness means the ultimate consciousness. And meditation is the bridge that takes you to the very source of your being. Once you have tasted the joy of being at the source, then everything else in life becomes meaningless. Then you can go on living an ordinary life, but it is all acting, it is a beautiful drama. Play it as well as you can, but you know now that you are not part of it. It is just a role; it is not your existence.

DAY 255

Life can become a total yes, but we have to change the whole pattern. All your no's can be melted and remolded into yes's. It is not as difficult as people think. Certainly it is not impossible. It has happened to many people – to Buddha, to Zarathustra, to Jesus, to Pythagoras, to Dionysius, to Lao Tzu. Around the globe it has happened to many people; it can happen to you. It should happen to everyone. In fact, we are here for it to happen. And that's what I call the shift from a prose lifestyle to a poetry lifestyle, a shift from mathematics to music. Then life is a song, a tremendous ecstasy.

I don't teach a religion of sadness. I am against all those sado-masochistic religions. I teach a new kind of religiousness which is rooted in love, not in fear, which is rooted in the present, not in the future, which is rooted in love and not in logic.

DAY 256

A man can live life either as a no or as a yes. If you live your life as a no, you become a warrior; you are constantly fighting. Then life is just a struggle, a war, and you are fighting against everybody else. Of course it is a losing war, you are bound to lose. One cannot win against the whole; the whole idea is stupid. But it appeals to the ego. The ego always wants to say no. No is nourishment for the ego. Love wants to say yes; yes is nourishment for living.

Love and ego are just polar opposites: if you say no, you make your ego bigger and bigger. The more ego you have, the less is the possibility of love. Without love, there is no joy; without love, there is no music; without love, there is no poetry in life. Without love, life is a desert. One can fight as much as one wants but it is self-destructive. Yes is creative, yes is the way of the creator, the way of the lover. Yes means surrender. If no means war, then yes means surrender: surrendering to the whole, trusting the whole as a friend – there is no need to fight – trusting life and existence. The moment you trust, you can relax, you can be in a let-go.

DAY 257

Ordinarily, people live a closed life. They don't open their doors and windows. They live in fear, hiding, always afraid of the unknown. They don't allow the sun, the rain, the wind to enter their being. But if you put a rose plant in your room and you close all the windows and all the doors, and no wind, no rain, no sun reaches it, you cannot hope that the rosebush will survive; it will die. That's how people are – almost dead.

They are living a dead life, just dragging somehow.

To really live, one has to be available to all that is. One has to be open and vulnerable. One has to drop all fears. There is only one thing to be afraid of, and that is fear. Except for that, never be afraid of anything because fear cripples, kills. The moment you start moving toward the unknown, in spite of all the fears, your life starts discovering many new things of which you were never aware: as the adventure deepens, your thrill, your ecstasy deepens too.

As you start moving into the unknown, there are so many challenges to be faced, encountered, that naturally you become more aware, more alert, more conscious. You have to be. It is walking on a razor's edge: how can you be sloppy? You have to be cautious and alert. It is risky. And whenever there is risk, your intelligence becomes sharp. When intelligence is sharp, ecstasy is great and you are thrilled at each movement. At each step, your inner being starts unfolding.

Only in this climate of adventure, ecstasy, integrity, risk, danger, intelligence, awareness, does the inner being open. The bud becomes a flower.

DAY 258

The moment you are not afraid of the unknown, the unknown immediately knocks on your door. If you are afraid, then it does not disturb you. Existence never interferes in anybody's life because it loves its creation. So it leaves everybody total freedom, even to go against it – that is part of freedom; even to close the doors – that is part of freedom; even to deny existence – that is part of freedom.

But it is foolish to use freedom in that negative way. Use freedom in a positive way, use freedom to receive the unknown guest, use freedom to create trust and love and bliss, so existence can penetrate you. And the meeting between your being and the being of the whole is the beginning of light, the beginning of eternal life, the beginning of immortality. That is the search that everybody is on, knowingly, unknowingly.

DAY 259

If you choose the old, you choose misery; if you choose the new, you choose bliss. Let this be a key: always choose the new, the unknown, the dangerous, the insecure, because it is only through risking that one grows. And growth is bliss, maturity is bliss.

Never for a single moment cling to the old. Go on dropping whatever is old. That moment it is old, be finished with it, put a full stop to it. Never look back; there is nothing worth looking back at. One cannot look back, one has to go ahead, always ahead. And be adventurous.

DAY 260

The most beautiful thing about danger is that it gives you alertness, awareness; hence the people who go climbing unknown peaks, unmapped, are really seeking awareness. They are not aware of what they are searching for. The people who have traveled to the North and South Poles, taking all kinds of risks, the people who have gone to the moon, are not aware of what their search is really for. They are searching for awareness, but not consciously.

A meditator goes consciously. There is no need to go to the Himalayan peaks or to the moon because there are higher peaks within you and greater distances within you and far more significant stars within you; the whole sky is there, the whole cosmos is there. But it is far more risky than going to the moon or going to Everest. The greatest, the most dangerous, the riskiest space is within; hence very few people dare to go there.

DAY 261

On the outside, remain joyful with the momentary; don't ask that it should be eternal. Nothing can be eternal on the outside. Enjoy the momentary as momentary, knowing perfectly well that it is momentary. The flower that has opened in the morning is bound to die by the evening. It has come with the sunrise, it will go with the sunset.

So rejoice! I am not against the flower – rejoice! But remember, don't cling, don't hope; otherwise you will be disillusioned. Rejoice in the momentary on the outside, and search for the eternal in the inside.

DAY 262

Man is a ladder – there are many possibilities in him and that is both a danger and a dignity, a glory and an agony. It is easy to fall: falling is always easier, no effort is needed for it. To rise needs effort. The higher you want to rise, the more effort is needed. If you want to reach the peaks of consciousness, you will have to risk all.

One should not take one's being for granted because man has no being at all – just a spectrum of possibilities, the whole spectrum. That is the beauty of man, and his misery too. He is the only anxious animal in existence, the only animal who feels anguish. The root cause of his anguish is that he is always at the crossroads. He has to choose at the crossroads. He has to choose every moment: to be or not to be, to be this or to be that.

DAY 263

Remain in the world but remain absolutely untouched, unidentified. That's what sannyas is all about: living in the world and yet not being in the world; living in the world, but not allowing the world to live in you; passing through the world fully aware that it is all momentary, so you need not become disturbed, you need not be distracted.

Then calamities and blessings, failure and success are all the same. And when you can see that darkness and light, life and death are all the same, a tremendous tranquility, equilibrium, balance happens to you. That profound silence is truth.

DAY 264

To live within limitations is to live in gloom, in a state of indignity. It is a humiliation because our being needs the whole sky, only then can it dance, can it sing, can it *be*. Otherwise everything is crippled, paralyzed: there is no space to fly, no space to move. And man lives in limitations: the limitation of the body, the limitation of the mind, the limitations of emotions, moods. These are all limitations upon limitations. And all these limitations have to be transcended.

That's the function of meditation, to help you to go beyond all boundaries. It is a voyage into the unbounded. Then all glory is yours; then life is a benediction, a sheer festivity, a pure joy. And to me, joy is the only thing that is godly because it brings all other godly qualities – love, truth, consciousness, silence. It brings everything that is needed, that is a requirement for spiritual growth. Without joy, nobody can grow. In misery one shrinks; in joy one expands.

Man should never be content with any boundary. Whenever you come to a boundary, try to go beyond it. When all boundaries are transcended, when you have reached infinity, you have come to existence – you have come home.

DAY 265

The lotus grows out of mud – the most beautiful flower grows out of dirty mud. It means that dirty mud contains something beautiful. So don't reject it, it contains lotuses. One has to know the art of growing lotuses. And it is a miracle – one cannot believe it! If one has not seen a lotus growing out of the mud, one cannot believe it. One cannot conceive that this beautiful flower, this delicate flower, with such fragrance, with such color, has come out of ordinary mud.

Man is born as ordinary mud, but contains a lotus – just as a seed. Man has not to be rejected, man has to be accepted and transformed. The world has not to be denied; it contains something infinitely beautiful. It is not on the surface, it has to be brought to the surface.

Hence I am not against anything: not against the body, not against the world, not against the outside. I am not against anything, but I am for transforming everything. Whatever existence has given is something valuable; if we cannot understand its value it is our fault, our limited vision.

DAY 266

Concentrate all your energy on meditation, so that you can learn the secret. It is a knack. Just by doing all the meditations, one day you will find which meditation fits with you. And the moment it fits, something clicks. Suddenly you know: "This is the method for me." And the knowing is so absolute and categorical that no doubt ever arises.

Then move with that meditation; let that meditation become the most central thing in your life because you will be born into light through it. And light is another name for godliness.

DAY 267

Learn from the birds their song, learn from the trees their dance, learn from the rivers their music. And once you open up you will be surprised: the whole of existence is such a poetic phenomenon!

One need not inquire into the meaning of it all; that becomes a philosophical inquiry. The moment you ask "What is the meaning of this?" you have lost track of the poetry. The moment you start dancing with a tree without asking "What is the meaning of this swaying tree in the wind?" you are being poetic. And the miracle, the miracle of miracles, is that the person who does not care about the meaning immediately finds it.

Dance with the trees, sing with the birds, swim in the ocean, and you will find the meaning without seeking it. Just become part of this beautiful existence. Sing your song: everybody has come with a song in the heart and unless you sing it, you will remain unfulfilled. You have to do your thing – that's what I mean by singing your song.

DAY 268

When you are silent your potential speaks to you, whispers to you. And those whisperings are absolutely categorical – there are no ifs and buts. The heart knows nothing of ifs and buts, it simply says that this is your destiny: become a painter or a poet or a sculptor or a dancer or a musician. It simply says to you that this is how you will be fulfilled. It starts directing you.

The function of the master is to help you to be silent so that you can hear your own inner whisperings and then your life starts moving through an inner discipline. So I don't give you any outer discipline. I help you to discover your insight; then you are free, then you move in freedom.

DAY 269

Don't think that some things are mundane and others are sacred. For the man who knows how to rejoice, everything is sacred. There is no division between the world and God – it is all divine. Perhaps the world is manifest God, and God is the unmanifest world. And when one rejoices, why make any difference between the manifest and the unmanifest?

The flower is the manifest seed and the seed is the unmanifest flower – they are one. So is this world and that, this shore and that. There is no need to divide materialism and spiritualism – they are both together. So rejoice in the smallest things: taking a shower or drinking tea. Don't make any divisions. To the man who knows how to be blissful, drinking tea is as sacred as any prayer can be, his sleep is as sacred as any religious activity.

DAY 270

A song simply represents a state in which one is open and ready to pour one's heart into existence. The song is symbolic – one is not miserable. The birds singing in the morning… Just like them, one has to be constantly in the mood for singing, as if it is always morning, as if it is always the time for the sun to rise.

Any moment the sun can rise and you have to welcome it, so you have to be in a receptive mood. You have to be alert – the guest can come at any moment. The singing birds are just getting ready to welcome the sun. The flowers start opening, the trees start swaying. The whole earth becomes alive, aflame, ready to receive a new day.

The singing heart, the dancing heart, the loving heart, is ready to receive godliness. The miserable can go on praying, but out of misery the prayer goes wrong from the very beginning. It becomes heavy and falls back down to the earth. It has no wings; it cannot go to the ultimate, it cannot reach God. When one is blissful, loving; when one is full of laughter, joy; when one is not serious about life, but playful like a small child – innocent, wondering about each and everything, looking at everything with awe – when the heart is singing hallelujah, then God can come any moment.

There is no need for you to go anywhere, just learn how to be receptive, open, loving, singing, cheerful – and he is bound to come. There is no need to become a Christian or a Hindu or a Mohammedan, there is no need to go to any church, to any temple or mosque. If your heart is overflowing with cheerfulness and love, there is no need to even believe in God, he is bound to come.

DAY 271

The most fundamental thing is to know the nature of existence so that we can be in tune with it. Otherwise everybody is out of step, and that being out of step is what misery is. To be in harmony with existence is bliss, to be in deep accord is bliss. To be in discord with existence is misery. So the only thing which can bring a total transformation in your life is to become aware of the truth, the nature, the Tao of existence. And the way does not go on the outside, the way goes through you; it is an inner journey.

First you have to find your own center. The moment you have found your own center you have found the center of existence because they are not two. We differ only as circumferences, at the center we are all meeting and merging. At the center we are all one: the trees, the mountains, the people, the animals, the stars. The moment you penetrate your own center you come to know the Tao of all that is. And once you have known the Tao, nature, the dharma, you cannot go against it. That will be simply suicidal. But without knowing it of course one is bound to stumble, bound to go astray.

Meditation is a way to find your center.

DAY 272

So many people seek and search for God without ever
bothering about whether they are ready to meet him, whether
they are ready so that he would want to meet them. They never
think about that. My emphasis is: forget all about God, just prepare yourself. Whenever the time is ripe and you are ready, God
is going to happen to you. You need not bother, you need not
even think about God; your thinking is not going to help.
Prepare – and to prepare means to rejoice, to blossom, to dance,
to sing, to love, to meditate, so that all the dimensions, all the
petals of your being start opening.

DAY 273

Bliss is an experience. I can teach you how to experience it,
I cannot tell you what it is. If you become silent, still, calm and
quiet and collected, you will experience it. Bliss is the experience of a silent state of mind, because in a silent state of mind,
mind disappears. It is no longer mind; it becomes no-mind.

And with the disappearance of the mind all desires disappear, all tensions disappear, all anxieties disappear. These are the
barriers which do not allow the flow of bliss in you, otherwise
bliss is your nature.

DAY 274

Man builds his life on the sands of his dreams. That's why
whatever one tries to do, everything fails, all houses collapse.
They don't have their foundation in something eternal; they are
founded in the momentary. And when one's house of sand falls
down, we start making another house – of the same material,
with the same material. We never seem to learn the lesson: if
one dream fails, we start dreaming another; if one desire is

frustrated, we immediately jump into another desire, another project – but we never see that desire as such is bound to fail.

To desire means going against the whole. It is an impossible task: it cannot be done. Not to desire means relaxing with the whole, going with the whole, having no desire of one's own. It means: "Whatever the whole wills is my will. I am not trying to achieve any individual goal." The moment you start trying to achieve an individual goal, you are bound for trouble because we are not separate from the whole, hence we can't have separate goals. The English word *idiot* is very significant in this context; its root meaning is: one who is trying to achieve something individual. He is an idiot because his failure is absolutely certain. Nobody has ever succeeded in achieving an individual goal. We have to learn to be part of life, existence. We are waves in the ocean: we cannot have individual goals and there is no need to at all.

DAY 275

We are not separate from existence, but we all live with the idea that we are separate. The idea of separation is the ego. The idea – just the idea – creates hell because then we become afraid for our own survival, become afraid for the future, we become afraid that one day we will have to die. It is all concerned with the idea of the ego. We don't understand that we are one with the whole, that there has been no birth and no death. We have always been here, part of the whole. It is just like a wave which rises in the sea; it was there in the sea even before it rose – and when it has gone back to the sea to rest, it is still there. Birth and death are both false; the wave remains, sometimes latent, resting, sometimes manifest, but it is there, it is always there. It is part of the ocean.

We are also part of this existence, we are waves of this ocean, and once this is understood, all anxiety disappears; there is nothing to worry about. This is our home – we are part of it.

There is no way for us to be anywhere else or not to be – there is no way at all.

DAY 276

Bliss is something very natural. If you stop creating misery you are blissful; it is not something that has to be invented by you. It is the same energy that becomes misery. Don't invest it in misery at all. Don't put your energy into jealousy, into hatred, into anger, into possessiveness. Withdraw it from all those stupid things.

William Blake is right when he says "Energy is delight." If you withdraw your energy from all stupid investments you are so full of energy, throbbing with energy, dancing with energy, you cannot contain it. You have to dance, you have to rejoice! You have to love, you have to laugh. It starts overflowing.

DAY 277

Every child in the mother's womb is blissful. He has nothing there – he is not the president of the United States, he is not the richest man of the world, he possesses no palaces – he has nothing at all, but his bliss is infinite. The psychologists say it is the bliss of the womb that haunts man all his life: how to regain it? We have tasted something in the mother's womb and we cannot forget it. We make every effort to forget it but somehow it lingers. It has been such a deep experience it is impossible to erase it. But it can be attained again very easily. One just has to become like a small child and think of the whole universe as the mother's womb.

That's actually what religion is supposed to do: to help you to think of the universe as the mother, so there is no conflict with you and the universe, so that you can trust the universe, so that you know deeply that it cares about you, that you need not be worried and need not be continuously anxious, tense, that everything is taken care of. Then suddenly there is great bliss. Meditation just helps you to fall back in the womb of the universe.

DAY 278

Truth is known only through a deep inner harmony. Ordinarily we are a chaos, very discordant, there is not one person in us but many. We are multipsychic; there are many minds inside, and they are all dragging us in different directions – many voices and you cannot figure out which is yours. One voice says "Do this," another voice says "Don't do this." You are constantly wavering, almost broken into thousands of pieces like a mirror thrown on the floor. That's the situation man finds himself in. But all those fragments can be gathered. They can be melted into the whole; they can be integrated, crystallized. That's what sannyas is all about: it is the science of crystallizing your fragments into one organic unity. The moment unity arises in you, great music is born. All the noises change into an orchestra, and only then can you see, hear, feel the truth of existence. It is always there but our minds are so noisy that we cannot feel it.

The moment this inner chaos is gone we can hear the still, small voice within. And then indubitably, unmistakably one knows, "This is my voice, this is existence speaking in me." And there is never any doubt. Even if the whole world doubts it, you will not doubt it: it is indubitable. Only on that rock of indubitability, on that rock of certainty, can life become a temple – otherwise we are simply making sandcastles.

DAY 279

We are not to become perfect, we are born perfect. And we are not to invent bliss, we have only to discover it. Hence it is not such a difficult matter as people think; it is a very simple process of relaxing, resting, and slowly, slowly becoming centered.

The day you stumble upon your center, suddenly all is light; you have found the switch. It is just like groping in a dark room: you go on groping and then you find the switch. And that's actually the situation. We are unnecessarily crying and weeping; hence those who have known have a very strange feeling about people. They feel great compassion and also great laughter because they can see the stupidity: you have already got it, but you are running hither and thither for no reason at all. And because of your running you go on missing.

Those who have known have great compassion too because you are suffering – that is true, although your suffering is simply foolish. It is like a man who has seen a rope as a snake and now is running away and falls on a banana skin, and breaks a few bones and may be in the hospital. You know that he was simply a fool – there was no snake at all! He could have even died from a heart attack – and without any snake; just a rope did the whole trick. This is the rope trick!

And that is the situation of man. This absurd, ridiculous life pattern has to be changed completely. Look within, and then, if you cannot find anything there, look outside.

But I say categorically that nobody who has looked within has ever missed it, so there is no reason for you to miss it. Nobody is an exception, it is an absolute law: one who goes within, finds it – finds the Kingdom of God, the perfect bliss, the absolute truth. And with it comes freedom and great fragrance.

DAY 280

One can create hell, one can create heaven – it is our own decision, it is our own responsibility.

All the good things in life – in fact life itself – are a gift of existence. So the problem isn't how to seek them, but how to receive them. Take bliss – or receive bliss – for example. It is not somewhere else far away in Tibet, in the Himalayas. It is not a question of traveling to it; the simple question is how to become more receptive. The gift goes on coming, but finds our doors closed. The sun rises, but we go on sitting in darkness because our eyes are closed. The gift is there – it is only a question of opening our eyes and all is light.

DAY 281

There are people who have become experts in finding reasons to be miserable. They cannot be happy unless they are miserable. They know only one happiness and that is that of misery. And when such people talk about their misery you can see in their eyes, in their faces, in the way they are talking about it – everything shows that they are enjoying it, they are bragging about it. They must be magnifying their misery, making it look as big as possible. Now how can these people ever be blissful?

And each moment always has both alternatives; you can choose to be miserable or to be blissful. Start looking at it in this way: in each situation, first try to find out what will make you miserable and what will make you happy about it.

DAY 282

When I was a small child, my father made a beautiful house. But the architect deceived him – he was a simple man – so the house collapsed in the first rains. We were just going to move into the house; just two or three days more and we would have been in the house and the house collapsed. My father was far away; I telegrammed him, "Come immediately, the house has collapsed." He never came, he never answered. He came when he was expected to come and the first thing that he told me was, "You are a fool! That house is gone – why did you waste ten rupees in sending me such a long telegram? Those ten rupees could have been saved! And thank God that the house collapsed at the right time. If it had waited just four or five days more, then it would have killed the whole family!"

He invited the whole village for a feast. I loved that idea. The whole town laughed saying, "This is sheer nonsense: your house has collapsed, everyone is feeling miserable about it." And he called all the people of the town – it was a small town – for a big feast, to thank God for helping us: "Just four days more and the whole family would have died!" This is what I call choosing the blissful part in every situation.

One of my sisters died. I loved that sister the most and I was miserable because of her death – although I had ten other brothers and sisters. My father told me, "You are unnecessarily disturbed about it. Thank God that you have ten brothers and sisters still alive! He could have taken all. What can we do? Just as he has taken one, he could have taken all. He has taken only one out of eleven. That is nothing, that much we can afford. We can give one child to God; if he needs her, let him have the child. But you have ten brothers and sisters – be happy that ten are still alive, rather than being unhappy for the one who has died."

This has to be the approach of every religious person. Then your life naturally becomes a blessed phenomenon.

DAY 283

Love is prayer, love is worship, love is religion – all else is bullshit! All else is just invented by the crafty priests to exploit humanity, otherwise it is a very simple phenomenon. The priest is not needed at all, these great rituals in churches and temples are not needed at all, but millions of people are exploiting others.

There is a certain need in man to seek and search for the truth. Because of that longing, man is available for exploitation; otherwise religion is a very simple phenomenon, no complexity at all.

Make yourself a lover of existence in all its manifestations.

Then you are neither a Hindu, nor a Christian nor a Moham- medan. Then you will find sermons in stones. You will be sur- prised that there is really no need to look into the religious scriptures because the whole universe is the real scripture. Everywhere there is existence's signature on it and all those so-called religions are man-made.

DAY 284

To be sad is to be a sinner, to be cheerful is to be a saint. If you can laugh wholeheartedly, your life starts becoming holy. A wholehearted laugh is something unique. Nothing can make your laugh more holy than a wholehearted laugh. And when you laugh, let all the cells of your body laugh with you.

From the head to the toe let the laughter spread. Let it reach to the deepest, innermost recess of your being. And you will be surprised that one comes closer to existence more easily through laughter than through prayer.

DAY 285

Just today I was reading about an old man, ninety-five years old. He was asked what the secret of his long life and his health was. He said, "I feel a little embarrassed to say the truth. The truth is that I have been getting my life from the trees. I hug them and suddenly subtle flows of energies start entering my body. They have kept me alive and full of juice." My own obser- vation is that he is right. He may not be able to prove it scien- tifically, but sooner or later it will be proved scientifically: if you love a tree, the tree responds; if you love a rock, even the rock responds.

Experiment with love in as many ways as possible and you will become richer every day. You will find new sources and new ways to love, new objects to love. And then ultimately a moment comes when one simply sits with no object of love, simply loving – not loving to somebody, just loving, just full of love, overflowing with love. And that is the state of enlightenment. One is fulfilled, utterly contented, one has arrived. The feeling, the constant feeling that something is missing is, for the first time, no longer there.

And that is the greatest day in one's life, when you can feel nothing is missing, nothing at all. You search and you cannot find anything missing, all is fulfilled.

DAY 286

When you see a beautiful sunset and you feel joyous, you naturally think that the joy is arising out of the beautiful sunset. That is not true. The beautiful sunset has simply triggered a process of meditation in you: It is so beautiful that your thinking has stopped. You are in a state of awe; it has possessed you. And the moment thinking stops, you fall into deep meditation and you touch the source of joy within.

DAY 287

Tomorrow should be tomorrow, never today. You should not expect it to be the same as today. That very expectation is dangerous because in the first place it is never going to be so; hence you will feel frustrated. And if, by chance, by accident, it happens to be just like today, then you will be bored, but neither frustration is joy nor boredom is joy.

Let the future be open. Don't put any expectations on it. Leave it unknown, unpredictable, and don't try in any way to make things permanent. The nature of life is change, and we have to flow with nature, with Tao, with the ultimate law of existence. Be in tune with it without any expectation on your part and you will be enriched tremendously. Each moment will bring you new joy, new life, new light, a new godliness.

And a person whose love is always flowing and who is never confined by anything becomes vast, as vast as the sky itself. In that vastness one knows what godliness is. That vastness is godliness.

DAY 288

To live in the present is the only way to live at all. And when you live in the present with no past dragging you backward and no future dragging you forward, when your total energy is concentrated in the moment, life takes on a tremendous intensity; it becomes a passionate love affair. You become aflame with your own energy, you become full of light because at a certain intensity, fire becomes life, intensity becomes light.

And that's the only way to be rich, to be prosperous.

DAY 289

The only way to be rich is to become available to existence, to all the colors, to all the rainbows, to all the songs, to all the trees and flowers, because God is not to be found in churches – churches are manufactured by man. God is to be found in nature.

You will find him in the stars, you will find him in the earth. When it rains for the first time and the beautiful fragrance arises out of the earth, you can find godliness there. You can find God in the eyes of a cow or in the giggling of a child. You can find God everywhere except the places that priests have invented. Churches, temples, mosques – these are empty, as empty as people are. Just be vulnerable, be soft and open, don't create a hard shell around yourself as a protection. Remain unprotected, insecure – and then the Kingdom of God is yours.

The moment one is ready to accept life as it comes, with no conditions, suddenly godliness rushes toward one from every nook and corner. To be full of godliness is the only possibility of having any meaning, any significance in life.

The person who has known godliness has known immortality. And then only the body will die; the essential core of his being is going to remain forever and forever.

DAY 290

The whole of existence has only one desire and that desire is for bliss. Hence I say bliss is God and there is no other God. All other gods are man's inventions, and it is better we drop them so that we can look in the right direction.

DAY 291

Love is the only bridge to victory. But it is a very strange bridge because the first requirement of love is surrender. It is victory through surrender; hence it has a tremendous beauty. It is nonaggressive, it is receptive; it wins not by conquering, it wins by being conquered.

Those who are trying to conquer existence are fools, they cannot do it. The wise people have surrendered to existence; they have invited it to conquer them. Existence cannot be possessed by you, but you can allow it to possess you. That's what love is: it allows one to be possessed. It is nonpossessive, it has no desire to possess. Its only longing is to be possessed, totally possessed, so nothing is left in oneself of one's own.

DAY 292

Life is not meaningless; it has intrinsic value. But it has to be discovered. We are unconsciously, intuitively, instinctively aware of it. We have just a hunch that there is bound to be some meaning – but we are not clear about it. It has not come to light; we don't have any proof of it. Love gives us proof of it. A lover has no doubts about life's meaningfulness, its significance, its joy. It is only through love that people have slowly, slowly discovered the ultimate meaning, godliness.

It is only through love that they have discovered the whole science of meditation because in loving moments, mind stops. When you are really in love, in those moments you don't think. The past disappears, the future disappears, the present becomes all and all – and that's what meditation is. Love gives you a glimpse of meditation, and through meditation a window opens into the existence of godliness; hence I call love the most godly phenomenon on earth.

DAY 293

Love is the highest form of poetry – and by poetry I don't mean anything literal. To me, poetry is far more than just composing poems. Poems can be composed even by someone who has no poetic life, who has no poetic grace. He can compose poems because to compose poems you only need a certain technique. He will be a technician, not a poet; and out of one hundred poets, ninety-nine are technicians. The same is true about every art: out of one hundred musicians, there is only one who is a musician; ninety-nine are just technicians. And it is so about sculpture, painting, architecture, every dimension of art.

The real poet has no necessity to compose poetry – he may, he may not. A real painter may paint, may not paint, but his life will be very colorful, his life will have a proportion, a symmetry, a balance. He himself will be his painting, he himself will be his poetry, he himself will be his sculpture.

That's what I mean when I say love is poetry: it gives you a new dimension; it makes you more aesthetic. It makes you aware of many things of which you were not aware before. It makes you aware of the stars and the flowers, and the green and the red and the gold of the trees. It makes you aware of people, their eyes, their faces, their lives. Each person is a tremendous phenomenon with infinite possibilities. Each person is an incredible story, each person is a living novel. Each person is a world unto himself.

DAY 294

Much is possible, but it has to be made possible. All that is needed to make it possible is available but one has to work consciously on it. It is as if you have plenty of land and plenty of seeds and plenty of water and sun, but you never sow any seeds in the field. Flowers won't come and your land will remain a desert. Grass will grow, weeds will grow.

That is one of the most important things to remember, that all that is useless grows on its own, and that which is significant has to be worked out. To achieve the significant is an uphill task. If you don't do anything weeds will grow; they will fill the whole ground. But then you cannot hope for roses and that was the promise.

Everybody comes as a great promise but very few people fulfill that promise.

DAY 295

You cannot exist without the whole, and the whole also cannot exist without you. Just that you *are* is proof enough that existence needs you in some way; you are fulfilling a certain need.

Even the smallest blade of grass is as needed as the greatest star. There is no hierarchy in existence. Nobody is higher, nobody is lower, and nobody is more needed and nobody is less needed. All is needed because existence means the togetherness of all. We all contribute something to existence, and existence goes on giving us everything we need. Once this interdependence is understood, life starts having a new kind of beauty and grace. Then there are no problems. Problems are created by the ego; because the ego is a false entity, it creates problems. It lives in anxiety, fear, always afraid, always cautious: something may go wrong...

The moment the ego is dropped, nothing can go wrong. Nothing ever goes wrong: all is perfectly right as it is. That's exactly the meaning of existence – that everything is good as it is.

DAY 296

All that is great in life happens only when you are courageous enough to put the ego aside, when you can stand in your total nakedness, hiding nothing, being nothing, being nobody. Then miracles start happening. Then love comes in, rushes in, fills you, and starts overflowing from you. And ultimately love itself becomes your experience of existence, your experience of truth.

DAY 297

The journey begins in love and ends in light or in enlightenment – and the bridge is prayer.

The whole pilgrimage from ignorance to wisdom is nothing but a pilgrimage of prayer. Prayer means: "I am so small that nothing is possible through me unless the whole helps me." Prayer is a surrender of the ego to the whole – surrender not in despair but in deep understanding. How can the small wave go against the ocean? The very effort is absurd. But that's what the whole of humanity is doing. We are all small waves in the vast ocean of consciousness. Call that ocean of consciousness God, truth, enlightenment, nirvana, Tao, dharma – they all mean the same thing, that we are part of an infinite ocean. But we are very small waves – we cannot have our own will and we cannot have our own destiny. The very desire to have our own will and to achieve something out of our own desires is the whole cause of misery.

Prayer means that in understanding the futility of human will, one surrenders to the divine will. One says, "Thy will be done, thy kingdom come." It is possible only if there is great love for existence. Hence I say the journey begins in love and ends in enlightenment. And the middle of the journey consists only of prayer, of deep let-go.

DAY 298

Now two thousand years have passed since Jesus, and humanity needs a quantum leap again. It is just a slight change: Jesus says God is love, I say love is God. That miracle is possible. When you say God is love, you make God more important than love. God may be many more things too; love may be only one aspect. God can be wise, God can be omnipotent, God can be omniscient, God can be omnipresent. God can be thousands of other things; out of those thousands of qualities, love is just one quality.

But my experience is totally different: love is God – God is secondary, love is primary. In fact, godliness is only one of the aspects of love, not vice versa. We can even drop the idea of God and nothing is lost. If one loves, that's enough, because love automatically brings a quality of godliness to your being, something of the beyond and the divine.

DAY 299

Religion is not theology, it is love. Theology is nothing but logic; hence it is called "logy." And logic has nothing to do with religion, in fact it is against religion.

Logic is a mind exercise, hair splitting, word chopping. It

can create beautiful wordy edifices but they are just castles made in the sand; they are of no use. They can keep you occupied, they serve the same purpose as when you are sitting on a beach and you start playing with the sand and making sandcastles just because you have nothing else to do. You can enjoy the occupation, but it is not beneficial at all, it is childish.

Theologians are never mature people. Jesus is not a theologian, neither is Buddha. No real master has ever been a theologian, but he is a lover, a tremendous lover. He loves the whole of existence. Love is his prayer, love is his worship, and through love, existence can be communicated with, you can have a dialogue. All that is needed is a deep love affair, a mad, mad love affair.

DAY 300

I don't teach any creed, I only help my people to be more conscious of everything that is within and without. That contains my whole teaching: be conscious, be aware and live out of your awareness. Let your awareness be decisive. Don't impose any discipline from the outside; let it spring from within, let it well up. And then it is always fresh, young, alive. And life becomes more and more intense, passionate; it becomes tremendously aflame with joy, with bliss and benediction.

DAY 301

Blessed are the blissful because they have already entered the Kingdom of God. Not knowing that they are entering God's heart, they have entered. In fact, God can never be found directly. You cannot approach God directly. He has no address; he has no name either, no form. If you search and seek God you will never find him. It is because of this fact that humanity has slowly, slowly turned atheistic, because people have looked for God and they have not found him. They searched, they wasted their lives, and finally they discovered it had been an exercise in utter futility.

But the whole responsibility falls on the shoulders of the priests, the popes, the *shankaracharyas*, the imams, the ayatollahs, the so-called religious people. They go on telling people to search for God, to seek God – and that is patent nonsense! I say seek bliss and you will find God. Seek God and you will not find him – you will become more miserable than you ever were, because not finding something on which you have staked your whole life is bound to make you very frustrated. Forget all about God; just search for bliss. Find the causes of your misery and drop those causes, remove those causes by the very roots. And you will be surprised: as all the causes of misery are dropped, bliss starts growing in you. And in blissful moments you will become aware of a new presence surrounding you – and not only you but the whole of existence. That presence is God. God is not a person but a presence. God is not God but godliness.

DAY 302

Bliss is something of the inner, absolutely individual, personal; you can find it within yourself – nobody else is needed. And once it is found, you are victorious. Then life has a great splendor. Then the whole sky of your being is full of stars.

And when one knows that one has not lived in vain, then even death is beautiful. One does not die reluctantly, one dies absolutely blissfully. Then death is just a rest.

One has blossomed, one has released one's fragrance; now the time has come to rest, to disappear in the whole.

DAY 303

The most significant thing about bliss is that it is intrinsically a paradox, and because of its paradoxical nature it has almost always been misunderstood. The paradox is that man needs to make great effort, and yet it does not happen because of effort, it always happens as a gift of existence. But without effort, man never becomes capable of receiving the gift. Even though the gift is always available, man remains closed.

So all the human endeavor is not really the cause of attaining bliss; it cannot cause bliss, it can only remove the barriers. It is a negative process. It is as if you are living in a closed room, all the windows, all the doors are closed: the sun has risen, but you are in darkness.

The sun cannot rise because of your efforts. Whatever you do cannot make the sun rise, but you can open your doors or keep them closed – that much depends on your effort. If you open the doors, the sun becomes available to you; otherwise it waits just on your doorstep, without even knocking. You can live in darkness for eternity – and all that was needed was to remove the barrier between you and the sun. Exactly the same is the case with bliss.

Existence is always showering bliss, it is its nature. Bliss is intrinsic to existence. It is not something that happens once in a while, it is not seasonal; it is its intrinsic nature, its very innermost core.

DAY 304

Learn to be more and more aware: aware of your body, aware of your mind, aware of your heart – aware of your actions, thoughts and feelings. These are the three dimensions to which awareness has to be brought. And when you are aware of all three you will become aware of the fourth – that is awareness itself.

DAY 305

Man seems to be the only animal that does not learn from experience at all. That is my observation. Even donkeys learn. In Arabic they have a proverb that even a donkey will not fall in the same ditch again – but can man do that miracle? He can fall in the same ditch thousands of times, what to say of twice or thrice? As many times as he passes by the side of the ditch, he will fall in! He will say to himself, "Let us try once more – maybe things have changed, maybe it is not the same ditch, and certainly I am no longer the same person. So much has changed; last time it was evening and this time it is morning. And what is wrong in it? One more try…" This is certainly the most important observation about man, that he never learns from his experience. He goes on in a vicious circle; he functions like a machine.

To be on the path of bliss, all that is needed is to learn from your experience. Don't repeat the same stupid things – the same anger, the greed, the jealousy, the possessiveness. Don't repeat them. You have repeated them enough and you have burned your hands enough. It is time to be aware, to be watchful, to be alert, and not to fall into the old traps again and again.

As you become capable of watchfulness, you become more and more capable of being free of all those traps. A moment comes when one is absolutely free from all traps and imprisonments – that is the moment of bliss. Bliss starts showering like flowers from the sky, and it goes on showering. One's life becomes a blessing to oneself and a blessing to others too.

DAY 306

Ordinarily you are not ready to receive; your doors are closed, your heart is closed. Even if existence shouts you won't listen. Existence goes on knocking on your doors, but you never open them; in fact, you don't think there are any doors.

You go on living your ordinary, mechanical, unconscious life. Effort is needed to make you conscious – but effort can only make you conscious, it cannot give you bliss. Whenever you are blissful, that means something has descended from above.

Those who have attained bliss have felt that their efforts have cleaned their hearts, opened their doors, removed all the barriers. And then one day, suddenly, something starts pouring from the beyond, from some unknown source. And when you look back you can see that your efforts were very tiny. You cannot say this tremendous ecstasy is an outcome of your tiny efforts; still they were needed, they were essentially needed, they cannot be avoided.

DAY 307

Our roots are in our center. If we are weeds, those roots are in the center; and if we want to become roses, we have to grow the roots of rosebushes in the center. Then the circumference will come to know the foliage and the flowers and the fragrance.

But you cannot move from the circumference to the center; the movement is always from the center toward the circumference. The circumference is just a shadow. And it is because for thousands of years, religious people, moralists, and all kinds of reformists have been trying to change the circumference that they have created a mess of humanity; the center remains the same.

The roots are of weeds and on the circumference we are hoping roses will come – they never come. Or, if we are very cunning, then we can purchase plastic roses and decorate the circumference. We can deceive others and finally we can deceive ourselves too. But plastic flowers are not real flowers. That's what the so-called moral character is: just plastic, synthetic. Real character has not to be cultivated, it is not to be practiced; it comes as a natural consequence of meditation.

DAY 308

Die to be reborn! That's the meaning of the Christian symbol of the cross. But Christians have missed the meaning of the symbol, as all religions have missed the message of the founders.

Buddhists have missed Buddha, Christians have missed Christ, Mohammedans have missed Mohammed. It is a very strange phenomenon that the followers are doing something totally opposite.

They go on calling themselves Christians but they are really killing the very spirit of Christ. Christ was not crucified by the Romans and the Jews. They could not kill him, they only killed the body. But if you want to know where exactly he has been crucified, the place is the Vatican: he has been crucified there by the popes. They have been continuously killing him.

The cross has nothing to do with a literal meaning, the cross simply means meditation. It simply means dying to the ego; hence the story that Jesus is resurrected after three days. Between death and resurrection there is a gap of three days. Those three days simply represent the body, the mind, and the heart.

First the body dies. You start dropping the idea of a separate body; you can see the stupidly of it. Each moment, existence goes on pouring new energy into you – how can you think yourself separate? If your breathing is cut off, you will be dead! And it is not only breathing; every day you are taking in food and water, every day you are dropping out everything that has died; life goes on pouring in and dead things are thrown out of the body. The body is like a river, continuously getting more life and dropping all that is dead. That represents the first death, the first day.

Then the mind, which is a little subtler, thoughts – they also come from outside. Just as air and water and food come from the outside, your mind goes on collecting thoughts from every-where. The mind dies as a separate entity.

And then the most subtle thing happens on the third

day – these three days are just symbolic – feelings, emotion, the heart dies. Then there is resurrection. In the East we call it the birth of the fourth, *turiya*: *turiya* means the fourth. When these three have disappeared, have become one with existence, suddenly you become aware of a being which is not yours, which is universal. That is resurrection.

DAY 309

Meditation is not doing at all, it is pure awareness. But a miracle happens, the greatest miracle in life. If you go on watching, tremendous and incredible things start happening. Your body becomes graceful, your body is no longer restless, tense. Your body starts becoming light, unburdened; you can see great weights, mountainous weights, falling from your body. Your body starts becoming pure of all kinds of toxins and poisons. You will see your mind is no longer as active as before; its activity starts becoming less and less and gaps arise, gaps in which there are no thoughts. Those gaps are the most beautiful experiences because through those gaps you start seeing things as they are without any interference of the mind. Slowly, slowly your moods start disappearing. You are no longer very joyous and no longer very sad. The difference between joy and sadness starts becoming less.

Soon a moment of equilibrium is reached when you are neither sad nor joyous. And that is the moment when bliss is felt. That tranquility, that silence, that balance is bliss. There are no more peaks and no more valleys, no more dark nights and no more moonlit nights: all those polarities disappear. You start becoming settled exactly in the middle.

DAY 310

When all desires disappear, you will not come back into the body, but you will remain in the universal consciousness as part of infinity. That's what we in the East call nirvana, the ultimate state of consciousness: when there is no need for a body, no need to be imprisoned again. We call it the ultimate freedom because to be in a body is a bondage. Of course, it is a very limited thing and you are unlimited: it is forcing the unlimited into such a limited, small world of the body. That's why there is constant tension, uneasiness, and one goes on feeling crippled, one goes on feeling crushed, crowded, imprisoned, chained.

One may not be exactly aware of it, but everybody vaguely feels that something is wrong. This is what is wrong: we are infinite and we are trying to exist through the very small world of the body.

Awareness frees you from the body. And the moment you know you are not the body, in that very moment all desires that can be fulfilled through the body also disappear. It is like bringing light into a dark room – darkness disappears. Awareness functions like light and desires are nothing but darkness.

DAY 311

My whole effort is not to give you a formal kind of religion, not to give you a church or a dogma to cling to, but to give you a new being, a new humanity, a new consciousness. One has to pass through two things. The first is a death, the death of the old, the death of the past, the death of the way you have lived up to now. And the second is a rebirth.

Start afresh, as if you were born today. It is not only a metaphor, it is so. You are born today. Let this sink deep into your heart so that you can become discontinuous with the past. Then the night is over and the sun has risen on the horizon.

DAY 312

Whenever the heart falls in love, the mind says "It is blindness," and whenever the heart calculates, moves in any direction, the mind always finds fault with it. They have different worlds. The heart's calculations are not logical, they are intuitive; it jumps from one point to another. And the mind goes through a detailed process, step-by-step. The mind thinks the heart is a fool and the people who live through the heart are thought by the mind to be fools. Jesus was called a fool in his life. Saint Francis was called a fool in his life, so much so that he started calling himself a fool – why bother others!

The heart always feels the mind is nothing but a Jew: always calculating, arithmetical, mathematical, calculating, cunning, clever; it knows nothing of simplicity, innocence, love. It is always counting money, always thinking in terms which are absolutely worldly. The heart has a deep condemnation for the mind; it looks on the mind as mundane. And the mind has a deep condemnation for the heart; it looks on the heart as mad, insane, foolish, childish.

And the body has its own way; it consists of its own way. The mind thinks celibacy is good, it can prolong your life, it is religious. And the body laughs deep down: "Go on thinking that, and I will show you when the time arises. I will see how long you can remain celibate. I will create so much trouble." It does create trouble and the mind has to bow down to the body. And this conflict continues, this is a triangle in which everybody is caught.

The whole process of meditation is to help all these conflicting forces to meet, merge, become harmonious with each other. Then you are so full of energy because all that energy that was wasted in unnecessary conflict becomes available to you. And it is that energy which becomes wings and takes you to the beyond.

DAY 313

Take all the responsibility for your life. If it is ugly, feel responsible for it. If it is nothing but anguish, take responsibility for it. In the beginning it is hard to accept "I am the cause of my own hell," but only in the beginning. Soon it starts opening doors of transformation, because if I am responsible for my hell, then I can create my heaven too. If I have created so much anguish for myself, I can create so much ecstasy too. Responsibility brings freedom, and responsibility brings creativity.

The moment you see that whatever you are is your own creation, you are freed from all outer causes and circumstances. Now it is up to you: you can sing a beautiful song, you can dance a beautiful dance, you can live a life of celebration. Your life can be a constant festival and nobody can disturb it. This is human dignity.

DAY 314

Truth means experience. Truth is never a belief. Beliefs are always lies. They can make your life a little bit more convenient, that's all; they are like tranquilizers. Truth is awakening. And man needs awakening, not tranquilizers to fall into a deep sleep. But for centuries, man has remained attracted to alcohol, to other kinds of intoxicants, to psychedelic drugs; from the time of the Rig Veda up to now he has remained addicted. In the times of the Vedas, he was addicted to soma and now he is addicted to LSD – there is no difference. All these intoxicants, psychedelic, alcoholic or whatever they are, are just efforts to avoid the truth.

To avoid the truth is to remain in misery. Yes, we can make a life which is surrounded by misery a little comfortable, but it is stupid. We can have an absolutely blissful life, but it is possible only if we drop the lies and inquire into truth. And the first requirement of the inquiry is not to carry any a priori ideas. Move in absolute ignorance, knowing nothing. Whenever a person moves in a state of not knowing, he is bound to know truth, and truth brings bliss.

DAY 315

It is not only that we are hiding our physical nudity behind clothes, that is nothing – we are also hiding our reality behind many, many layers. We want to appear beautiful and we hide ugliness; we want to appear knowledgeable and we hide ignorance. But remember, whatever you hide you will remain; you will remain that which you have hidden inside. You will never be that which you are pretending to be.

It is better to drop all hypocrisy. I don't teach renouncing the world, I teach renouncing hypocrisy. That is the only thing to be renounced; everything else happens on its own. Be sincere, authentic, true. Whatever you are, accept it, because without accepting it you will not expose yourself. The healing is always done by existence, but you have to allow it: you have to show your wound, where it hurts. You don't deceive the physician; you have to tell him, whatever it is, and however ugly it appears. You have to show your wounds; only then can the pus be taken out, only then can existence help the healing process.

DAY 316

By creating a character, one becomes false, and split also. One becomes two people because the very method of creating a character is that of repression – there is no other way. You have to repress your nature and you have to act according to certain principles decided by others. They tell you what is right and what is wrong, what is good and what is bad. They have already given you Ten Commandments and you have to follow them. Now what will you do with your nature?

The only thing possible is that you repress your nature, you neglect it, ignore it. But nature cannot be changed in this way; it goes on nagging you from within and forcing you to go against the character you have cultivated – hence all the hypocrisy. It is very rare to find a religious person who is not a hypocrite. And only a person who is not a hypocrite is really religious.

Hypocrisy means you pretend to be something which you are not. You know it, it hurts; hence there is sadness. The whole world is full of sadness because the whole world has been directed to create character, morality. My effort here is just the opposite. I am not interested in character at all, in morality at all. I am not telling people to be immoral; I am telling people to be conscious, to create consciousness. And that's what meditation is meant for. It is a method to create consciousness. It makes you more alert, more aware, and as you become more aware your life starts changing.

DAY 317

Man has lived for centuries in lies – beautiful lies, but all lies. We go on believing in heaven and hell, we go on believing in God, in immortality, in the soul, but these are all beliefs – and beliefs are lies. You don't know anything on your own, whether there is a soul within you or not. And it is not a question of argumentation: even if it is proved logically that you have a soul, it will not make any difference to the quality of your life. Or if it is proved there is no soul, that will also not make any difference.

There are theists, there are atheists, and they are all living almost the same life, the same stupid life, with no qualitative change. There are people who believe that God exists and there are people who believe that God does not exist, but if you look into their lives there is no difference. So what is the point of all these arguments? It is futile. The only thing that matters is experience, not argument.

If you don't even know whether the soul exists within you or not, what else can you know? How can you know God and heaven and hell and all that nonsense? The closest thing to you is your soul, and you have not even explored that! And you are talking about some heaven somewhere above in the sky, and some hell deep down. You have no idea what you are talking about. In churches and temples and mosques, people are continually arguing, discourses are being given about great things, and nobody bothers about the most simple thing – knowing who you are.

DAY 318

People live in comfortable lies. They don't want truth, they want consolation, cozy consolation; hence they remain clinging to superstitions, to traditions, to conventions, because all that is old has a certain prestige, a certain credit in the marketplace. All that is old, they say, is gold. It is not so: the old looks gold only to fools, to cowards.

Life is new every moment, it is never old. Existence is always now and here. It has nothing to do with the past and nothing to do with the future either. The moment you are also now and here, there is a meeting – and that meeting becomes the truth. Of course it will shatter many illusions, it will shatter many ideologies. It will shatter all your conceptions, all a priori beliefs, because truth cannot fit with you, truth cannot compromise with you and your ideas about it. You have to be ready to fit with truth.

That's what I call a love for truth: a readiness to go with truth wherever it leads. And whatever needs to be dropped, one is ready to drop. That is possible only if there is love for truth. Love can do everything, love can sacrifice everything. And truth requires total sacrifice, total commitment.

DAY 319

Modern man is living in such a hurry that he cannot sit, he cannot rest. He has become incapable of rest. And once you are incapable of rest, you are incapable of all that is valuable. The reality is that we need not be so worried about anything. Life is eternal. We have always been here and we always will be here; we are immortals. The body is going to change, the mind is going to change, but we are neither: neither the body, nor the mind.

It is only in deep meditation that we discover the simple fact that we are not the body and the mind, we are awareness, consciousness. We are the witness of the whole game. Once you have known that witness, you have tasted something of the nectar that the alchemists were in search of.

DAY 320

We have to de-automatize ourselves, we have to become slowed down in every act. So you have to be aware: when you are walking, don't walk at the old pace, with the old speed; slow down, so much so that you have to be alert, otherwise you will gather speed again, which is automatic.

Buddha insisted that his disciples walk very slowly, for the simple reason that if you walk very slowly, you have to be constantly alert. The moment you lose track of alertness, you start walking the old way, you go fast. The machine starts functioning again. He used to tell his disciples to breathe very slowly, for the simple reason that if you breathe very slowly, you will have to be conscious of it.

So do everything very silently, very slowly, very peacefully, gracefully, so that each act becomes a deep meditation in awareness. If we can transform our acts into meditation, if meditation can be spread all over our lives, from morning to night… The moment you wake up, remember the first thing: get out of bed, but be very alert. You will forget many times in the beginning;

remind yourself again and again. Slowly, slowly one gets the knack of it. Once you have the knack of how to be aware in your day-to-day life, you have the secret key. And that is the most important thing. There is nothing more valuable than that secret key.

DAY 321

The whole past has been dominated by sad people. Sad people very much enjoy dominating others. They have no other joy; their only joy is crushing other people and their freedom, their only joy is in making more and more people joyless. They are very jealous and angry with people who are happy, who can sing and dance and rejoice. These sad people have destroyed so much that it is almost inestimable. Nobody has done as much harm to humanity as these people – and these are the popes, the *shankaracharyas*, the ayatollahs, the imams. The priests of all the religions have been against humanity.

My effort here is to create a new man, and a new man can be created only with a new vision; a new man is possible only with a new vision of religiousness. I teach a religion of love, laughter, celebration. It is my own experience that you are bridged with existence when you are blissful. So I teach bliss and bliss and nothing else.

DAY 322

Remember two words: one is *gravitation*, the other is *grace*. Gravitation is the law of the earth, it pulls things down. Grace is the law of heaven, it pulls things up. Science discovered gravitation; religion discovered grace.

Ordinarily we are born and live under the law of gravitation. Our whole life is a downward pull. We begin in birth and we end in death. We begin fully alive and we end as a corpse.

This is the downward flow. Unless one starts moving inward, the grace, the second law, cannot function. If we remain identified with the body, then the law of the earth prevails; the body is part of the earth.

When we start moving inward – that's what meditation is all about – we become aware of something which is not part of the body. It is in the body, it is not the body. The body is only a temple, it is not the deity. Once you have become aware of the inner deity that resides in the body, the second law immediately starts functioning: you are pulled upward. Life becomes more and more abundant, more and more rich, more and more infinite, more and more perfect. It moves toward the sky, it starts becoming as vast as the sky, even the sky is not the limit. But the secret is in meditation.

DAY 323

The body has a limitation, it is confined between life and death; and so is the mind. Mind is not separate from the body. It is its inner aspect; the inside of the body is the mind, the outside of the mind is body. All the languages have to be changed sooner or later as far as the words *body* and *mind* are concerned. Languages give the false idea that these two are separate entities. It is not like *body* and *mind*. The truth is *bodymind*. It is one word, it is one reality. Just as every coin has two aspects and every wall has two sides, so is the case with bodymind. The body is limited, the mind is limited; hence the fear of death.

The body cannot be afraid because it is unconscious, but the mind can be afraid. The mind is constantly trembling. The fear is that sooner or later the full stop is going to come. And more than the full stop, the problem is that we have not achieved anything yet, and life is going down the drain; every moment death is coming closer and life is slipping out of our hands. Hence the fear, the anxiety, the anguish. But beyond the bodymind complex, fortunately, there is something more in us too – and that is consciousness. The consciousness is unlimited, it is oceanic, it is vast. The bodymind is just like a dewdrop and the consciousness is like an infinite ocean. The bodymind begins at the time of birth and ends at the time of death, but the consciousness has no beginning, no end.

To know this consciousness is to be free from all fear, anxiety, anguish. To know this consciousness is to become deathless, eternal, timeless.

DAY 324

Ordinary courage is not enough, total courage is needed because one almost has to die, to die to the past so that the new can be born. It is a rebirth. But it can be managed, it is not impossible. We have the potential to do it.

Existence requires of you only that which you *can* do; it never requires anything impossible, difficult – arduous, of course, but not impossible. It is tremendously paying. When one moves from the mind to no-mind, one is passing through death deliberately. The thrill is immense and the surprise is infinite.

For the first time, one starts experiencing life in its utter beauty. That experience is godliness.

DAY 325

Transformation is possible only when the twenty-four hours of your day become a constant meditation, a continuum. So whatever you are doing – walking you are meditating, eating you are meditating, listening, talking, you are meditating. To me, meditation simply means awareness, not repeating a mantra. Because how can you repeat a mantra? If you are working and you repeat a mantra, your work will be disturbed. If you are doing something significant, then it can be dangerous to you; you will be divided.

By meditation, I simply mean awareness. Whatever one is doing, one is fully aware of each act – physical, mental, emotional. Walking, you are aware of walking; running, you are aware of running; swimming, you are aware of swimming. Eating, you are not simply stuffing yourself unconsciously and thinking of thousands of other things: you are simply eating and doing nothing else at that moment, totally in the act, alert, aware. Then meditation becomes a twenty-four-hour-a-day phenomenon.

One day a miracle happens, and that miracle is that one can sleep with meditative awareness. The body sleeps, but somewhere deep down a current of awareness continues: you are aware that you are asleep. A very paradoxical phenomenon, but it happens. On that day, meditation has come to its completion, is known in its entirety.

DAY 326

It is not accidental that old people become very bitter. It is very difficult to live with old people, even if they are your own parents. It is very difficult for the simple reason that their whole life has gone down the drain: they are feeling bitter. They jump upon everything to throw out their negativity. They start catharting and freaking out over anything. They cannot tolerate children being happy, dancing, singing, shouting out of joy – they cannot tolerate it. It is a nuisance for them because they have missed their lives. And in fact when they are saying "Don't be a nuisance to us," they are simply saying "How dare you be so joyous!" They are against young people, and whatever the young people are doing, the old always think they are wrong.

In fact they are simply feeling bitter about the whole thing called life. And they go on finding excuses; it is very rare to find an old person who is not bitter. If there is an old person who is not bitter, that means he has lived really beautifully, he is really grown up. Then an old person has tremendous beauty that no young man can ever have. He has a certain ripeness, maturity, he is seasoned. He has seen so much and lived so much that he is tremendously grateful to existence. But it is very hard to find that type of old man because it means he is a Buddha, a Christ, a Krishna.

Only an awakened person can be non-bitter in old age – because death is coming, life is gone, what is there to be happy about? One is simply angry. You have heard about angry people, angry young men, but really no young man can ever be as angry as old people. Nobody talks about angry old men, but my own experience – I have watched young people, old people – is that nobody can be as angry as the old.

Bitterness is a state of ignorance. You have to go beyond it, you have to learn the awareness which becomes a bridge to take you beyond. And that very going beyond is revolution. The moment you have really gone beyond all complaints, all no's, there arises a tremendous yes – just yes, yes, yes – there is great fragrance. The same energy that was bitter becomes fragrance.

DAY 327

Evolution is an unconscious phenomenon. It is a natural phenomenon. The scientists say man was born as a fish in the ocean; millions of years have passed between the stage of the fish and that of the human being. Man had to pass through all kinds of animal stages – the last stage before man was something like the ape, the monkey.

All this has happened unconsciously; no deliberate effort has been made. But since man became man, that evolutionary process seems to have stopped. It seems to have come to its culmination, because man has been man for thousands of years and no further growth has happened. It shows one thing, that nature has done all it could do; now we have to take it in our hands. We have to move from evolution to revolution.

Evolution means unconscious, revolution means conscious. Evolution is growth, but because it is unconscious it takes millions of years. Revolution is also growth, but because it is conscious it is like a quantum leap, like a jump. It is not gradual, you don't go slowly step-by-step. It all depends on you, on how courageous you are. Even in a single step one can move from a human being to a god, to a buddha, to a christ – just in a single leap. It all depends on your intensity, your commitment, your involvement, your totality.

DAY 328

In a better human society, we will tell every child: "You have the seeds of love, of bliss, of truth, but they are seeds. Your whole life has to be a tremendous effort to sow the seeds, to learn the art of growing, to be patient, to wait for the seeds to sprout – then to take care of the plants and still to prayerfully wait for the right season when the flowering happens."

And that's what we are doing here. It is an experiment in inner farming, in inner gardening, in inner agriculture. But the first thing has to be the shock that up to now we have lived in vain, and that whatever you have done has been done from wrong ideas. We have to make the slate clean, so the whole past is simply put aside. A sannyasin has to begin from scratch. Sannyas is a new birth: it is as if you are born today and now you have to start living. Forget the past, don't go on carrying it. It has not given you anything. It has been tragic – no need to remain burdened with it. Become free of it so that you can experiment afresh.

DAY 329

Everybody is born blind and everybody has the capacity not to be blind. Everybody is born blind because at birth we are bound to be unconscious, unaware. It is only through life and its experiences, good and bad, painful and blissful, that one slowly,

slowly wakes up. It is only through a rich life – and by rich I mean a lived life. One who has been in the thick of life, one day becomes capable of opening his eyes.

In that very moment, one passes through a radical transformation. Then life is never the same again.

DAY 330

Man is blind, not because he has no eyes but only because his eyes are covered with much dust. That dust has to be removed and with the dust, blindness disappears. Man is like a mirror and it is natural to collect dust. All that is needed is a constant cleaning of the mirror. That's what meditation is all about, the art of cleaning your inner mirror of consciousness.

Meditation has to become just like eating, drinking, taking your bath, sleeping: a natural part of your life, of your ordinary life – nothing special, nothing spiritual, nothing to brag about. Only then, slowly, slowly blindness disappears; one becomes able to see.

DAY 331

The moment we are awake, all misery and all suffering looks so absurd, so foolish, so ridiculous, that one wonders "How did I suffer? And what was suffering? For how long I suffered – and it was all false. There was no substance in it; it was just an idea, a dream."

Hence the mystics call our world an illusion, maya. Remember, suffering is illusory, bliss is our true nature. Remember it again and again and again.

DAY 332

Man can exist in three ways: either like an animal or like a human being or like a god.

Ordinarily people live like animals; there is not much difference. The only difference is that man is worse than other animals; he can fall lower than any other animal. He is more cunning, more corrupt. He misuses his capacities. Rather than being creative he becomes destructive…

Adolf Hitler could have become a buddha, he had the same potential. Judas could have been a jesus, he had the same potential, the same energy. But energy is neutral; it depends on how you use it, how you decide and choose to use it. Life is your choice. You are free to choose, but you are not free not to choose: you will have to choose this way or that. Even choosing not to choose is a way of choosing. It is inevitable, you cannot avoid it. The people who exist on the lowest level are the people who have not chosen: choice means struggle, effort, it is an uphill task, so it seems better not to choose and to remain as one is born.

One is born as an animal. Very few become human beings. Humanity exists only in name, it has not yet arrived. Only those who have chosen, who have become decisive about their destiny, who have a sense of direction, who are creative, who are constantly discovering, exploring new ways of being and growth, who are not satisfied with the instinctive, who want to be intelligent in their lifestyles, are human. They are human beings.

DAY 333

Man lives mechanically, just like a sleepwalker, a somnambulist: he goes on doing things, but just like a robot. If you start watching your acts, you will be surprised that you go on making the same mistakes every day. You have decided many times not to do them again, but those decisions are meaningless. When the situation arises again, you react immediately in the old pattern: you don't know how to respond.

These two words are significant. *Reaction* means mechanical, unconscious, and *response* means nonmechanical, conscious. Response means according to the situation and reaction means acting according to the old pattern. Reaction means following ready-made answers, following an inbuilt program, being dictated and dominated by the past – that is reaction. And living in the moment, with no interference from the past, is response.

DAY 334

The only difference between the animal and the human is that the animal is absolutely unconscious, the human is a little bit conscious. And the only difference between the human and the divine is that the divine is absolutely conscious. Man exists between the absolute unconsciousness of the animals and the absolute consciousness of the buddhas, of the gods. One can either move downward, fall back into darkness, or one can start climbing.

DAY 335

The body consists of darkness and the soul consists of light. Where this darkness and light meet is the territory of the mind. So the mind has both a little bit of light and a little bit of darkness; hence the mind always remains in tension because it is being pulled in two opposite directions.

The body pulls toward itself, the soul pulls toward itself. And both are almost equal magnetic forces, so the mind remains hanging in between. Sometimes it chooses the body, sometimes it chooses the soul. But whatever it chooses, there is always the feeling that it is wrong because the other has been left out. There is a feeling that something is missing. The mind continuously lives in choice and every choice is going to be only half – the other half will take revenge. Hence mind is anxiety, anguish.

My whole effort is to help you to go beyond mind. The mind cannot become part either of the body or of the soul. One has to get out of the mind to be free of the tension. Unless one transcends the mind, goes beyond it, one cannot feel peace. There is no such thing as peace of mind. People talk about peace of mind – that is nonsense. Mind means no peace, no-mind means peace. So the right expression will be "peace of no-mind" – then you are centered in your real being.

DAY 336

The mind argues but never reaches any conclusion; the heart never argues and knows the conclusion. This is how it is; it is one of the mysteries of life. The mind is very noisy but all the noise is useless; the heart is silent but delivers the goods.

Move from the head to the heart, from argument to no-argument and life suddenly becomes a new phenomenon, full of significance and meaning, beauty and fragrance, full of light and love. And all these combined together is the meaning of godliness.

DAY 337

Thoughts are like darkness, they appear just like darkness appears. It looks so real, but just bring light in and it is no longer there. It is just an appearance, something very illusory.

That's why you cannot do anything directly with darkness: you cannot throw it out, you cannot bring it in. Absolutely nothing can be done directly to darkness because it does not exist in the first place. It has no weight – it is just an absence of light. So when you bring light in, because of its presence the absence disappears.

The same is true about the mind: the mind is the absence of

meditation. The moment you enter meditation, mind disappears just like darkness. And only then does one know that one has lived in a very illusory world. The mind is the world in which we live. The real world is far away from us. The mind is between us and the real, and it goes on distorting the real, interpreting the real, projecting itself on the real. It never allows you to see reality, it never allows you to see even your own self. It becomes so important that you become focused on it, and the two realities, the outside and the inside, both disappear. The non-substantial becomes your whole life; it dominates you. You live through the mind, you live as the mind.

And that's the only problem. To live in something illusory is to live in vain. There will be no growth, no maturity, no richness, no understanding, no bliss, no truth, no beauty.

DAY 338

It is only the loving heart that can touch the heart of existence. The mind is shallow and superficial; it knows nothing of the heights and depths. The mind is idiotic, it is always mediocre. It cannot give you any insight into reality. For that your heart needs to function – and love is nothing but the humming of the heart.

Allow the heart to sing its song. Even if the mind condemns it, don't bother about the mind. The mind will condemn it; it will say, "This is irrational." For example, when the situation suggests that you should be miserable but you start singing a song, the mind will say, "This is not right, this is not how things should be, you have to be miserable – that is logical." Somebody has died and you dance... That's what we do here. We just wait for an opportunity! People go on thinking, "Now who is next? Who are we going to celebrate next?" We don't miss any opportunity!

Once you allow the irrational heart to function, slowly, slowly the mind loses its grip. It will take a little time because the mind has been in power so long; it will condemn you, it will create trouble for you. Just listen to the heart and let the mind go on shouting.

DAY 339

The complaining mind can never be religious. It is impossible for the complaining mind to be religious, because the complaining mind has not become aware of a basic reality: that existence loves you, that it takes care of you, that you are befriended by the winds, by the rain, by the sun, by the moon. Whatever happens, it may appear a curse to you, but it is never a curse, it is always a blessing. Maybe in the beginning it appears like a curse because our vision is very limited, our perspective is very small. We can't see the whole thing, we can't see all the implications of it. We can't see the whole series of events that will be followed by it; otherwise we would always be grateful, we would always feel blessed.

Even in death, a man who understands finds tremendous thankfulness toward existence, because for him death is a rest. For him death is not the end of life, but the beginning of a far greater life than this one. This was just a rehearsal of the real life – it was not real.

The real drama starts after death – for those who understand. Those who don't understand think the rehearsal is the real thing, and when the rehearsal ends, they cry and weep, and they cling, and they don't want to leave it.

Everything is a blessing.

DAY 340

Meditation simply means becoming empty of all the contents of mind: memory, imagination, thoughts, desires, expectation, projections, moods. One has to go on emptying oneself of all content. The greatest day in life is when you cannot find anything to throw out – when there is only pure emptiness. In that emptiness you find your pure consciousness.

That emptiness is empty only so far as the mind is concerned, otherwise it is overflowing, overfull. It is full of being – empty of mind but full of consciousness. So don't be afraid of the word *empty*, it is not negative. It negates only the unnecessary luggage which is of no use and which you are carrying just from old habit, which does not help but only hinders, which is just a weight, a mountainous weight. Once it is removed you are free from all boundaries, you become as infinite as the sky.

DAY 341

Man needs a pure heart to commune with existence. The heart becomes pure when the mind is no longer dominant within you. While the mind dominates, the heart remains impure. The mind clings to the heart like dust clinging to a mirror. Mind is nothing but thought dust; each thought is just dust and nothing else. One has to clean all thoughts, then purity is attained.

Purity has nothing to do with morality. Of course a pure heart is moral, but a moral person need not be pure. A moral person is still living in the head; his morality is still a domination of the head.

The head is saying "Do this, don't do that." And the head is very calculative: it calculates about this world and it calculates about the other too. It does not know purity because it is not innocent; hence remember, morality does not lead to purity. The opposite is true: purity certainly leads to morality, but purity comes first, then morality follows.

DAY 342

Our real being is our innermost core, it is not somewhere outside. One need not go anywhere, one has simply to come back home. It is not a journey from here to there; on the contrary, it is a journey from there to here. We are already there and we have to be here. We are always then and we have to be now.

So whenever your mind starts moving somewhere, bring it back here. When it starts moving to the past, to the future, bring it to the now. Remember these two words: *now* and *here*. Slowly, slowly one starts living herenow, and that is the only way we can meet existence because it is always herenow. And we are never herenow. The moment we are also herenow, the meeting happens, is bound to happen.

DAY 343

Whenever you have time, close your eyes to the whole world and forget all about it. Shower your center with all your attention, care, love, and soon you will see flowers coming up. It is a kind of gardening, a kind of farming, and it brings tremendous joy because when you come to see the flowers of consciousness, you know that life has not been a waste, that you have not missed the opportunity – that you have used it.

DAY 344

The ultimate experience of life is a paradox. It is the sound of silence. Now, logically that is absurd: something can be sound or it can be silence – it can't be both together. But those who have known agree that it is the sound of silence, it is the sound of one hand clapping. All those who have known agree about the paradoxical nature of the ultimate reality because it contains the polar opposites. It is night and day simultaneously, it is life and death together.

Logic divides, experience unites. Logic creates opposites; experience makes you aware that there are no opposites at all, not at all. All opposites are just complementary.

DAY 345

The Western mind lives in time-consciousness, the Eastern approach is toward timelessness; hence the Eastern definition of truth is that which is beyond time. Unless you go beyond time, you know nothing of truth. In time you see just a film on the screen – it can be beautiful and for the moment you may become enchanted with it, but deep down you know it is just fiction. You may become engrossed in it, you may completely forget that it is just a fiction, you may start taking it for real – and if it is a three-dimensional film it can give you the notion, the feeling, that it is real. Then the end comes and just the screen is left; suddenly there is the realization that only the screen was real the whole time, and the film was just a projection.

The world of facts is just a projection; the screen is the reality, but it is hidden behind the projection.

The screen is God and the world is just a film moving on that divine screen. How to penetrate the real – that which is and will always be and has always been? The method that we have discovered in the East is meditation. Meditation simply means dropping all fictions and facts, cleansing the mind of fiction and facts so that only the screen remains. The screen of consciousness is pure and empty, clean and white, and nothing moves on it. All movement has disappeared because all movement is in time.

Time has stopped, the clock has stopped. Suddenly you are transported into another world, the transcendental world. And that is the world of truth. To know it is to know all, and to know it is to be it, because then the knower and the known are no longer separate; then the knower is the known, the seer is the seen, the observer is the observed. That is the ultimate experience which liberates, which liberates you from all the fantasies of the mind and from all the mundane facts of the world.

DAY 346

Reality is paradoxical; it contains all polar opposites in it. Seen in the right perspective they are not thought to be opposites, they start looking complementary. Hence the paradox is only from the lower world of thinking. When you yourself reach the peak of no thought, there is no paradox; you suddenly see the unity of all opposites. In the ultimate, the day and night meet and merge, life and death meet and merge, summer and winter meet and merge – there is no difference.

DAY 347

When you start meditating, you have to begin by watching the thoughts. Just by watching, one day they disappear. This silence of the mind, when thoughts disappear, is the first step.

Then begins the second step: the silence of the heart. That comes by watching the feelings. It is a more subtle phenomenon, far deeper than the first, but the process is the same. If one succeeds in the first, one will be able to succeed in the second too. It is the same method of watching. And one day, feelings disappear too. Then the second silence is achieved. And when both these silences are there, for the first time you know that the watcher also has disappeared because there is nothing to watch. And there is nothing to know, the knower disappears. That is the ultimate silence.

DAY 348

To be with a master simply means to live with someone who is awake, who is no longer asleep, whose dreams are finished, whose nightmares are over. And just being in tune with the master slowly, slowly wakes you up.

The very energy of the master starts penetrating your being.

Slowly, slowly it seeps into your heart; slowly, slowly it gives you a new heart, a new beat. And you cannot remain long with a master without becoming awake because he is continuously shouting, calling you forth to wake up, calling you forth to come out of your grave.

If you can open your eyes just once, suddenly for the first time you will experience the music, the song, the dance; and it goes on increasing, it goes on moving toward a crescendo, toward a height which is absolutely unimaginable to the ordinary mind. It is beyond the mind, far beyond; hence the mind cannot say anything about it. It is indescribable, indefinable. The mind simply falls short with all its logic, language, words, with all its efficiency as far as the world is concerned.

In the encounter with the beyond, the mind feels utterly impotent for the first time. The impotence of the mind releases a new energy in you. That energy I call the song, the dance, the ecstasy.

DAY 349

Everything is a gift. We have not earned it, we don't even deserve it. Seeing a beautiful sunset, have you ever pondered over the matter "Do I deserve it?" Listening to a distant call of the cuckoo, have you ever thought "Do I deserve it?" Or the wind passing through the pine trees or the river dancing toward the ocean and the sky full of stars – what have we done to have this beautiful universe? We have not paid for it, we are not worthy of it.

It is out of the experience that we don't deserve it, yet it has been given to us, that religious consciousness arises, gratitude arises. One starts feeling tremendously grateful to the unknown hands, the invisible hands that have created this beautiful, this tremendously, unbelievably beautiful existence. In that gratitude one is religious – not by being a Christian or a Hindu or a Mohammedan, just by being grateful.

DAY 350

The universe is vast, unbounded, and so are we because we are part of it. The part is indivisibly one with the whole, so whatever is the quality of the whole is the quality of the part too.

Just remember a very small formula: if all the parts are finite, then the total cannot be infinite. If the total is infinite, then all the parts must be infinite too. And we are part of this infinite existence. We are also infinite. Hence the Eastern seers have declared, "*Aham brahmasmi* – I am God." Al-Hillaj Mansoor says, "*Ana'l haq* – I am truth." These are tremendously important declarations. They have declared it on behalf of the whole humanity. These are not egoistic assertions, they are simply statements of facts. And just feel it: you are part of an infinite existence that begins nowhere, ends nowhere. You immediately feel uplifted, weightless. Your small worries and small problems drop. They become so insignificant compared to the vastness that you are. They lose all meaning, they simply become irrelevant.

DAY 351

Every awakened person has felt a tremendous compassion for people and tried his best, but something in the very experience is such that it cannot be expressed. If one wants to know it, one has to experience it: truth can only be an experience.

You are full of stars, full of flowers, but absolutely incapable of transferring it to anybody. It is nontransferable, it cannot be taught. But those who are alert can catch a glimpse of it. It cannot be taught, but it can be caught.

DAY 352

It is impossible to express the ultimate truth. It is like a taste. If you have tasted it, you know; if you have not tasted it, there is no way to convey it. A man who has not tasted honey cannot be made to know what sweetness is.

A man who has never seen light is incapable of understanding anything about light. Even the person who has known and experienced finds it almost impossible to express it because language falls very short. The experience is so vast and language is so small. The experience is so sacred and language is so mundane that there is no possibility of any bridging. Hence the truth has been known many times and all those who have known have tried to express it, but they have failed. But we are grateful that they tried because out of that effort life has been enriched.

DAY 353

Belief is death, it is a full point; you simply take it for granted. Somebody says something, somebody authoritative – the Bible, the Koran, the Gita – and you simply believe that authority. To believe in any authority is to destroy your own intelligence. All authorities are destructive of intelligence. I am not an authority in that sense. Whatever I am saying, I am saying according to my experience – that way I am authoritative, but that authority does not mean that anybody has to believe in it. That simply means: take it as a hypothesis and then inquire whether it is true or not.

Being here with me simply means exploring. And if you start exploring, you *will* find. There is no need to believe because it is so. "*Aes dhammo sanantano*" says Buddha – this is the truth, the ultimate truth. So if it is the ultimate truth, there is no need to believe; you can experience it.

Belief is insisted upon only by people who themselves don't know. They are afraid of inquiry, they are afraid of doubt, they are afraid of questions. They repress all questioning; they condemn all doubt. I respect doubt.

So I have to be just a hypothesis for you. I will give you hypotheses; then you have to go into inquiry. And I know you will find the truth because I have found the truth through the same inquiry. I trust everybody's intelligence and everybody's intrinsic potential.

DAY 354

Every person is born with a divine voice although we never hear it. It is a still, small voice. It is the voice of existence. But our heads are so full of other voices – and there are a thousand and one voices – that we can't hear the still, small voice.

In our heads, all the stations are on simultaneously. It is so noisy inside that even if existence shouts, you won't hear. And it never shouts, it whispers. Love always whispers because to shout is a little violent. Love knows to wait; hence existence waits. Love knows to hope, hence existence hopes. If not today, then tomorrow... Some day you are going to hear it.

DAY 355

The most unique experience in life is that of silence; otherwise life is very noisy. Outside there is noise, inside there is noise and both together are enough to drive anybody crazy. They have driven the whole world crazy.

One has to stop the inner noise – the outer noise is beyond our control and there is no need either to stop it, but we can stop the inner noise. And once the inner noise is stopped and silence settles, the outer noise is no problem at all: you can enjoy it, you can live in it without any problem. The experience of inner silence is unique, incomparable. There is no other experience which can be of much value, because out of that experience all other experiences grow. It is the foundation of the whole temple of religion.

Without silence, there is no truth, no freedom, no godliness; with silence, suddenly things which were not there are there, and things which were there are no longer there. Your vision has changed, your perspective has changed.

Silence makes you capable of knowing the invisible, of knowing the unknowable. That's its uniqueness.

DAY 356

Society has no interest in your love energy. Its whole interest is in your head, in your logical capacity, because that can be used as a commodity in the market. Society only wants you to be efficient – not meaningful, simply efficient, as efficient as a machine. But the machine has no idea of love and will never be able to have any idea of love.

As far as the head is concerned, sooner or later computers are going to replace it. What the head does, computers can do in a far better way. But I don't think that any computer is ever going to fall in love. Logic is a mechanical capacity and so machines can do it. Love is really the human element in you, but society is not interested in it, has no use for it; hence it teaches everybody to be logical. And the more hung up in the head you become, the more you forget your heart. My work here is to bring you back down to the heart.

DAY 357

My effort here is to help your love become greater. All the so-called religions have been trying just the opposite. Seeing that love creates misery they teach the renouncing of love. I also see that love creates misery, but seeing that, I teach the renouncing of limitations. Let your love become unlimited.

The so-called religious traditions and my approach begin from the same point but we move in different directions. They think it is love that is creating the trouble; I don't see that it is love that is creating the trouble. It is the limitation that you impose upon love that is creating the trouble. Renouncing love is not the solution. Renounce the limitations. Just be loving; let love be a spontaneous, natural phenomenon. Don't make it a relationship; relate but don't become confined to relationships. The moment you free your love from limitations, you are free. The moment your love is free, your very being is free because your being consists of love, your soul consists of love.

DAY 358

You have to live in such a way that when you leave the world, you leave it a little more beautiful than you had found it – that's enough! You have proved that you were religious. You have proved that you were not accidental. You have proved that you have contributed something to existence, that you have not been futile and in vain, that your being here has been of significance.

The very feeling: "I have contributed a little bit to the beauty of the world, to the grace of existence. I have added a little more light into the dark night of the soul" and one feels fulfilled, immensely contented. Nothing more is needed, no other religion. And creativity can come only out of meditativeness.

DAY 359

There are many people who are thought to be mad simply because they are heart people and they cannot communicate with the world which has been created by the head. Their only problem is that they are in a far better space than the rest of the world. It is like a man who has eyes living with people who don't have eyes: he will be in constant difficulty. Nobody will listen to him, nobody will ever understand him; he is inevitably going to be misunderstood, on each point, on each count.

Hence very few people dare to live in the heart. They are

the mystics; they have come very close – but to be close means still a little far away. One more quantum leap is needed, one more jump, and then you reach the indescribable.

DAY 360

Friendship has something spiritual about it. Love is biological; friendship is spiritual. And unless love becomes something like friendship, one suffers through it – rather than finding bliss, one finds more and more misery. But the reason is not in the energy of love. The reason is that you have not been able to refine it; you have not been very artful about it. You have taken it for granted, as if it is the end. This is not the end. Let your love become friendship; let your love become prayer. These are the two possibilities, two aspects. If you become friendly with the person you love, then you can love many people. Then your love spreads, then the circle becomes bigger and bigger. This is one aspect.

The other aspect is that when you start loving many people with no clinging and you also allow the others the same, your love starts growing another aspect – the aspect called prayer.

Prayer means loving the whole, the whole universe, becoming friendly with the trees and the rocks and the rivers and the mountains and the stars. When friendship reaches the point of prayer, one is religious.

DAY 361

The ego has to be totally dropped. You are not to be achievers. Whatever you need is already given, it is already the case. All that you need is to let it grow. Your potential is there; you have to remove hindrances. You can call my thinking "negative thinking" rather than positive thinking. Positive thinking says to project your idea of who you want to be; I say existence has already made you what you are, only negate the hindrances.

That has been the most ancient teaching of the great mystics, of all the buddhas. We call the method *neti-neti*. Go on saying, "This is not me, this is not me" and go on removing everything till nothing is left to be removed. When absolute nothingness has happened, in that nothingness, the lotus opens up. When you are not, for the first time, you are. And to experience this paradox is the greatest experience in life.

DAY 362

The really religious person is very earthly; he has to be, otherwise he won't have roots. Hence I teach rootedness to the earth. I teach the earth, because I know that only if our roots grow into the earth will we be able to rise beyond the clouds. The flowers will come, but they will come only through getting deeper and deeper roots.

So to me, the mundane and the sacred are not different; they are two sides of the same coin. Hence singing and dancing and love and creativity and cheerfulness and laughter are not against the sacred. They are part, an intrinsic part of it, and not a small part – exactly half of it, and the first half. If the first half is there, the second half follows automatically. They cannot be separated. But in the past, the second half became more important. And not only more important, it became empty of the first half. That's how religion died. That's how godliness died on the earth: godliness became a tree without roots.

Godliness can live again, but the only way for it to live again is to have roots in the earth – and that's what I mean by cheerfulness, song, celebration.

DAY 363

The lotus is very symbolic – it grows out of mud. The most beautiful flower grows out of dirty mud. Prayer grows out of sexuality, the soul grows out of the body – which is just mud – and godliness grows out of the world.

On the surface it looks impossible. If you look at mud, you cannot believe that it can produce lotuses. If you look at the lotus, you cannot believe that it can come out of dirty mud. But that's how it is; the lowest is connected with the highest. The highest is in the lowest and the lowest is in the highest: everything is bridged. And life is a ladder. That's my basic teaching: nothing has to be denied, not even the dirty mud. Everything has to be transformed into a lotus.

DAY 364

Man can live either in time or in eternity. Both alternatives are open because there is nothing like destiny, nothing like fate. Man is freedom: he comes without a fate. The future is open, always open, it is not determined when you are born – each act determines it. In each act is your choice, and on each step you can change the very direction of your life.

Millions of people live in time, for the simple reason that they are born in a crowd which knows nothing about eternity. Their parents have lived in time, their teachers have lived in time, their leaders have lived in time, the whole society around them lives in time, between birth and death; hence every child starts imitating. That's the way the child learns but that's also how he becomes conditioned.

It is rare phenomenon to get out of the rut of time, only a few people have managed up to now. Not even all the names which are thought to have escaped, not all the so-called saints and mahatmas and sages, not more than one percent of your so-called saints, have been able to escape the prison of time. Although it creates much misery, its walls are invisible; hence there is a desire and longing to get rid of misery, but you need great intelligence to see that the misery is bound to be there if you choose time as your lifestyle.

Time means change – and when everything is changing, you cannot cling to anything, you don't have any support, no security. There is no earth underneath your feet, you are on shifting sands. Hence one feels afraid, worried, anxious, and all this becomes the root cause of one's misery, despair, hopelessness.

But there is a way, and the way is not to fight with misery, the way is to get out of the wheel of time. In a way it is very simple, but sometimes the simplest thing, the very obvious thing, is missed because it is too obvious and our eyes are searching for something great, something far away – and it is very close by! Everybody has been told that time consists of three tenses – past, present and future – and that is absolutely wrong. Time consists only of past and future. The present is a penetration of eternity, the present does not belong to time; it is transcendental. To live in the present is to get out of time; to be here now, totally here now, is to be out of the wheel.

DAY 365

Who knows whether tomorrow one will be here or not? This is the way one has to live: each moment has to be the last moment, so why live life halfheartedly? You may not be able to live another moment, so put all that you have, risk all that you have in the moment, because who knows about the next moment. This is the way to live!

And when you don't care about the result you become a lotus. The lotus has to be remembered again and again so that you can go on getting deeper and deeper into the now and here – but unattached, unclinging, untouched. No future, so that you can live totally, and no past so that you remain untouched.

Once that happens, life is bliss – unbounded bliss, infinite bliss, eternal bliss.

about Osho

Osho's unique contribution to the understanding of who we are defies categorization. Mystic and scientist, a rebellious spirit whose sole interest is to alert humanity to the urgent need to discover a new way of living. To continue as before is to invite threats to our very survival on this unique and beautiful planet.

His essential point is that only by changing ourselves, one individual at a time, can the outcome of all our "selves" – our societies, our cultures, our beliefs, our world – also change. The doorway to that change is meditation.

Osho the scientist has experimented and scrutinized all the approaches of the past and examined their effects on the modern human being and responded to their shortcomings by creating a new starting point for the hyperactive 21st Century mind: OSHO Active Meditations.

Once the agitation of a modern lifetime has started to settle, "activity" can melt into "passivity," a key starting point of real meditation. To support this next step, Osho has transformed the ancient "art of listening" into a subtle contemporary methodology: the OSHO Talks. Here words become music, the listener discovers who is listening, and the awareness moves from what is being heard to the individual doing the listening. Magically, as silence arises, what needs to be heard is understood directly, free from the distraction of a mind that can only interrupt and interfere with this delicate process.

These thousands of talks cover everything from the individual quest for meaning to the most urgent social and political issues facing society today. Osho's books are not written but are transcribed from audio and video recordings of these extemporaneous talks to international audiences. As he puts it, "So remember: whatever I am saying is not just for you...I am talking also for the future generations."

Osho has been described by *The Sunday Times* in London as one of the "1000 Makers of the 20th Century" and by American author Tom Robbins as "the most dangerous man since Jesus Christ." *Sunday Mid-Day* (India) has selected Osho as one of ten people – along with Gandhi, Nehru and Buddha – who have changed the destiny of India.

About his own work Osho has said that he is helping to create the conditions for the birth of a new kind of human being. He often characterizes this new human being as "Zorba the Buddha" – capable both of enjoying the earthy pleasures of a Zorba the Greek and the silent serenity of a Gautama the Buddha.

Running like a thread through all aspects of Osho's talks and meditations is a vision that encompasses both the timeless wisdom of all ages past and the highest potential of today's (and tomorrow's) science and technology.

Osho is known for his revolutionary contribution to the science of inner transformation, with an approach to meditation that acknowledges the accelerated pace of contemporary life. His unique OSHO Active Meditations™ are designed to first release the accumulated stresses of body and mind, so that it is then easier to take an experience of stillness and thought-free relaxation into daily life.

Two autobiographical works by the author are available:
Autobiography of a Spiritually Incorrect Mystic,
St Martins Press, New York (book and eBook)
Glimpses of a Golden Childhood,
OSHO Media International, Pune, India

OSHO international meditation resort

Each year the Meditation Resort welcomes thousands of people from more than 100 countries. The unique campus provides an opportunity for a direct personal experience of a new way of living – with more awareness, relaxation, celebration and creativity. A great variety of around-the-clock and around-the-year program options are available. Doing nothing and just relaxing is one of them!

All of the programs are based on Osho's vision of "Zorba the Buddha" – a qualitatively new kind of human being who is able *both* to participate creatively in everyday life *and* to relax into silence and meditation.

Location

Located 100 miles southeast of Mumbai in the thriving modern city of Pune, India, the OSHO International Meditation Resort is a holiday destination with a difference. The Meditation Resort is spread over 28 acres of spectacular gardens in a beautiful tree-lined residential area.

OSHO Meditations

A full daily schedule of meditations for every type of person includes both traditional and revolutionary methods, and particularly the OSHO Active Meditations™. The daily meditation program takes place in what must be the world's largest meditation hall, the OSHO Auditorium.

OSHO Multiversity

Individual sessions, courses and workshops cover everything

from creative arts to holistic health, personal transformation, relationship and life transition, transforming meditation into a lifestyle for life and work, esoteric sciences, and the "Zen" approach to sports and recreation. The secret of the OSHO Multiversity's success lies in the fact that all its programs are combined with meditation, supporting the understanding that as human beings we are far more than the sum of our parts.

OSHO Basho Spa

The luxurious Basho Spa provides for leisurely open-air swimming surrounded by trees and tropical green. The uniquely styled, spacious Jacuzzi, the saunas, gym, tennis courts...all these are enhanced by their stunningly beautiful setting.

Cuisine

A variety of different eating areas serve delicious Western, Asian and Indian vegetarian food – most of it organically grown especially for the Meditation Resort. Breads and cakes are baked in the resort's own bakery.

Night life

There are many evening events to choose from – dancing being at the top of the list! Other activities include full-moon meditations beneath the stars, variety shows, music performances and meditations for daily life.

Facilities

You can buy all of your basic necessities and toiletries in the Galleria. The Multimedia Gallery sells a large range of OSHO media products. There is also a bank, a travel agency and a Cyber Café on-campus. For those who enjoy shopping, Pune provides all the options, ranging from traditional and ethnic Indian products to all of the global brand-name stores.

Accommodation

You can choose to stay in the elegant rooms of the OSHO

Guesthouse, or for longer stays on campus you can select one of the OSHO Living-In programs. Additionally there is a plentiful variety of nearby hotels and serviced apartments.

www.osho.com/meditationresort
www.osho.com/guesthouse
www.osho.com/livingin

more books and eBooks by OSHO media international

The God Conspiracy:
The Path from Superstition to Super Consciousness

Discover the Buddha: 53 Meditations to Meet the Buddha Within
Gold Nuggets: Messages from Existence

OSHO Classics
The Book of Wisdom: The Heart of Tibetan Buddhism.
The Mustard Seed: The Revolutionary Teachings of Jesus
Ancient Music in the Pines: In Zen, Mind Suddenly Stops
The Empty Boat: Encounters with Nothingness
A Bird on the Wing: Zen Anecdotes for Everyday Life
The Path of Yoga: Discovering the Essence and Origin of Yoga
And the Flowers Showered: The Freudian Couch and Zen
Nirvana: The Last Nightmare: Learning to Trust in Life
The Goose Is Out: Zen in Action
Absolute Tao: Subtle Is the Way to Love, Happiness and Truth

The Tantra Experience: Evolution through Love
Tantric Transformation: When Love Meets Meditation

Pillars of Consciousness (illustrated)
BUDDHA: His Life and Teachings and Impact on Humanity
ZEN: Its History and Teachings and Impact on Humanity
TANTRA: The Way of Acceptance
TAO: The State and the Art

Authentic Living

Danger: Truth at Work: The Courage to Accept the Unknowable
The Magic of Self-Respect: Awakening to Your Own Awareness
Born With a Question Mark in Your Heart

OSHO eBooks and "OSHO-Singles"
Emotions: Freedom from Anger, Jealousy and Fear
Meditation: The First and Last Freedom
What Is Meditation?
The Book of Secrets: 112 Meditations to Discover the Mystery Within

20 Difficult Things to Accomplish in This World
Compassion, Love and Sex
Hypnosis in the Service of Meditation
Why Is Communication So Difficult, Particularly between Lovers?
Bringing Up Children
Why Should I Grieve Now?: facing a loss and letting it go
Love and Hate: just two sides of the same coin

Next Time You Feel Angry...
Next Time You Feel Lonely...
Next Time You Feel Suicidal...

OSHO Media BLOG
http://oshomedia.blog.osho.com

for more information

www. **OSHO** .com

a comprehensive multi-language website including a magazine, OSHO Books, OSHO Talks in audio and video formats, the OSHO Library text archive in English and Hindi and extensive information about OSHO Meditations. You will also find the program schedule of the OSHO Multiversity and information about the OSHO International Meditation Resort.

http://OSHO.com/AllAboutOSHO
http://OSHO.com/Resort
http://OSHO.com/Shop
http://www.youtube.com/OSHO
http://www.Twitter.com/OSHO
http://www.facebook.com/pages/OSHO.International

To contact OSHO International Foundation:
www.osho.com/oshointernational,
oshointernational@oshointernational.com